Steve -

Thanks for your service to WSC!

Since you will soon have extra free time, I thought you might be interested in one physicist's slice through spirituality.

As leader of an interfaith alliance, you will recognize that there are many paths up Pikes Peak - but only one summit!

Best wishes on your future endeavors!

Lance

The Spirit of Reason

BEING AN INVESTIGATION OF TRUE AND FABULOUS THEOLOGY

L.L. Williams

First Edition

KONFLUENCE PRESS
Manitou Springs, Colorado

The Spirit of Reason
BEING AN INVESTIGATION OF TRUE AND FABULOUS THEOLOGY
by L.L. Williams

Published by *Konfluence Press*
a division of *Konfluence Research Institute*

ISBN, print edition: 978-0-9753995-1-4
Library of Congress Control Number: 2006922202

ISBN, online edition: 978-0-9753995-9-0

Contact for permissions, orders, or information:
Konfluence Press
P.O. Box 467
Manitou Springs, Colorado
80829

www.konfluence.org/press
press@konfluence.org

Historical quotations in Pilot Wave used with the permission of *Oxford University Press.*

πREFACE

It has been over 200 years since the great American Revolutionary Thomas Paine first wrote of the true and fabulous theology, although that grand message was somewhat overshadowed by his withering deconstruction of the "mythologies" of Christianity. Impervious to the controversy which ensued, Paine could afford to be bold. By then he had the fresh winds of the Enlightenment blowing at his back. The creation of the United States of America was a recent, glowing triumph of reason and of Enlightenment values.

Delighting in the depth and power of Newton's discoveries of mathematical physical law, Paine grasped the true revelation: it was the universe itself. The Creator does not write books, nor choose earthly emissaries. Instead, the Creator writes, godlike, in a scripture which sprawls across the sky.

Paine could not have known that the true and fabulous

theology since his time has revealed the fabric of our universe to be woven with a select few mathematical patterns. These patterns involve a corresponding few special numbers in their mathematical description. Each of these numbers contains a message rich in complexity and information content.

The best known of these special numbers is π, a number unmistakable to any citizen of this universe who has discovered the circle. The number π has been known on earth for thousands of years. For circles that are inches in size or kilometers in size, the ratio of the circumference to the diameter is always the number π.

To write this number as a Greek letter is to encapsulate a vast numerical expanse. Only the first 40 digits of π are written above; π goes on forever and does not repeat. It stores an infinite amount of information and has been calculated out to trillions of digits. Circumferences, areas, and volumes cannot be specified without it. The angles of a triangle add up to it. π is a numerical fingerprint of our universe.

It is a mystery why π has the value it does. But by its very nature π is an incontrovertible message from the Creator. We may not have understood the message, but we have certainly read it. Whatever message or meaning may lurk in π, it was written by the Creator.

The message of π is beyond reproach. It cannot be faked; it is not written by humankind. Knowing π is, strictly speaking, a revelation of the divine in the natural world.

Mathematics provides the key to seeing π and the other divine patterns wrought by the Creator in the physical universe. No priest is needed to read the divine message. One need only measure the ratio of a circle's circumference to its diameter. For humanity to be given the gifts to read and write the divine language of mathematics is nothing less than an act of grace

Although the peoples of earth find many things to argue over, the value of π is not one of them. It is the material world of nature, and our quantitative understanding of it, on which we can all agree. Engineers and scientists of all nations and religions recognize the same expressions of physical law. They recognize the same numerical value for π. There is a universal book of nature.

In contrast to the unity of humankind's understanding of the physical world, understanding of the spiritual world is fractured into many religions. Religious fundamentalists wage war in the physical world to settle arguments about the spiritual world. Prayers and longings to know God are not directed toward a common sky.

Yet the fundamentalists of many religions are joined together against a common foe: science. In the most technologically advanced nation on earth, almost 400 years since religious authorities condemned Galileo for teaching that the earth orbits the sun, and on the threshold of the 21st century, science still comes under attack where it challenges ancient superstitions and mythologies. This drama has recently been played out in the movements to suppress the teaching of biological evolution in public school science classes. These confrontations started soon after Darwin's theory became widely known, have been ongoing through the Scopes trial early in the last century, and continue today.

Perhaps the time has come for a new spiritual paradigm based upon the eternal truths reflected in the physical reality, truths such as π. Truth is to be sought in religions which see the universe as the body of the Creator and every speck of matter as divine. The mystery of Creation is as sublime as the mystery of the Creator. The physical realm of Creation is a source of magnificent spiritual insight. Because the physical universe gives birth to humans and humans give birth to spirit, human beings link matter and spirit. Human spirituality is an outgrowth of the divinity of the natural world.

The true bible is not written in a language of men. It is written in mathematics. The true bible of natural law is unencumbered by earthly intermediary. The books of this bible are numbered with the constants of mathematical physical law. The prophets of this bible are the great physicists. Their revelations are so profound as to challenge the limits of human comprehension. The universe itself is a divine revelation and the equations of mathematical physical law are its scripture. The message of the Creator is written in the very stars of the sky, the same sky we all share.

THE WORD OF GOD IS THE CREATION WE BEHOLD:
And it is in *this word*, which no human invention can counterfeit or alter, that God speaketh universally to man.

- Thomas Paine, *The Age of Reason*

Contents

Reason

No moment of human history was more profound than when Isaac Newton unleashed the Promethean fire of mathematical physical law. The subsequent decoding and understanding of the mathematical laws underlying our physical universe bestowed upon us a gift of sorcery. In an historical wink of an eye we ascended from cave dwellers to moon walkers.

That we may perceive and decode mathematical patterns embedded in the strata of reality is a gift of truly mythical proportions. The discovery of these mathematical patterns has conferred awesome power upon humankind. It is the power to guide the forces of nature and to know the history of the universe from the moment of its creation.

About 100 years after Newton's triumphal discovery of

mathematical physical law, Thomas Paine, in a series of pamphlets beginning with *Common Sense*, proclaimed *reason* as the basis of democratic governments. He saw the United States as the first modern government based on reason. The Declaration of Independence resonates with the words and ideas of *Common Sense*.

Paine rode the wave of success of the American Revolution to a position of eminence in the French Revolution. Unlike the American Revolution, the French Revolution turned violent against the Catholic Church because it was seen as an instrument of the monarchy. Paine was shocked to see the renunciation of spirituality in response to its association with a corrupt Church. To inspire and enlighten his fellow revolutionaries, he wrote *The Age of Reason.* His book on the spiritual power of reason was subtitled *Being an Investigation of True and Fabulous Theology*.

In gusts of inspiration, Paine critiqued the foundations of Christianity, Judaism, and Islam, challenging their legitimacy as spiritual doctrines. Paine intended to clear the underbrush of organized religion to make way for a spiritual doctrine unencumbered by human frailty. For Paine, it was a mistake to bind our natural compulsion to spiritual growth with mortal organizations. When the leaders of these organizations fail, they should not cause a lack of faith in spiritual potential, but instead create a recognition that the divinity may not have been in these organizations to begin with. He made clear where the real message of the Creator was to be found:

> It is only in the CREATION that all our ideas and conceptions of a *word of God* can unite. The Creation speaketh an universal language, independently of human speech or human language, multiplied and various as they be. It is an ever-existing original, which every man can read. It cannot be forged; it cannot be counterfeited; it cannot be lost; it cannot be altered; it cannot be suppressed. It does not depend upon the will of man whether it shall be published or not; it published itself from one end of the earth to the other. It preaches to all nations and to all worlds, and *this word of God* reveals to man all that is necessary for man to know God.[1]

The link from science to spirit was already forged when Jefferson and Paine spoke of the rights of men originating in "natural law". These were the inalienable rights, the rights that no monarch could confer or deny. People are imbued with certain fundamental rights by virtue of their very being.

Democracy is founded in principles beyond the control of men.

Reason is the divine basis for our approach to other people and to the natural world. The divinity of reason is self-evident. It is just and honest. It seeks harmony and seeks to understand. It is the presumption of goodwill among people. No individual is above another. All have equal rights and equal value. Tom Paine used the spiritual light of reason to illuminate a just system of government, and showed us how reason and spirit are connected.

Applied to the natural world, reason recognizes the existence of order and the repeatability of things. Through reason we make the measurements that allow us to understand the phases of the moon and the cycles of the heavens. Reason knows that nature is blind to human desire. Storms depend on changes in barometric pressure in America the same way they do in Asia. An electron has the same mass in Iran as in Indiana as in the farthest reaches of our galaxy. Nature reveals the same numerical result to quantitative measurement, indifferent to whether the experimenter be peasant or king.

To submit to reason requires the opening of hearts and

minds in a way that can only be described as spiritual. It is the recognition of the greater order, of a kingdom beyond men. Reason applied to social affairs has yielded the gifts of democratic governments and free markets. Applied to observation of the natural world, it has yielded quantitative understanding, which in turn has lead to mastery of the forces of nature. The powers of the magical hammer wielded by the Norse god Thor pale next to the powers unleashed by our mathematical understanding of physical law. Yet such understanding remains beyond the grasp of those who cannot reason – or who chose not to reason. These powers are achieved through neither faith nor incantation, but through reason and its expression in mathematics.

Emblematic of the power of reason is the number *e*, which is written to 40 digits in the page heading. Like π, *e* is a number that can never be fully written out. Its digits go on forever without repeating. Unlike π, which was first discovered in nature, *e* was *predicted.* It is a unique number which naturally arises in the mathematics used to describe physical law. It epitomizes pure reason. It is a number that was waiting to be discovered, a number written by God.

Adherents of many spiritual doctrines embrace a dialog with the Creator of a more qualitative nature: Will my dreams come true? Will my prayers be answered? What will happen to me after I die? What will be my reward or punishment? They are all compelling questions. Unfortunately, the answers to such questions vary among differing spiritual doctrines, often depending ultimately on faith and belief.

Mathematical physical law allows us almost any query of Creation. But in this dialog with the Creator, we can only ask questions whose answers are numbers. The question has to refer to the physical constituents of the universe such as planets, baseballs, battleships, movie stars, dinosaurs, or gamma rays. Past and future are also legitimate questions, but our dialog with the Creator must be *quantitative*.

While mathematics is of human creation, the patterns it describes are written by the Creator into the fabric of the universe. The striving to know physical law is a striving to know the mathematical Word of God. A mathematical universe was constructed and we were given the ability to discover it.

Perhaps this was part of the intended dialog between Creator and creation all along. As Paine said about this dialog with the divine, "It cannot be forged; it cannot be counterfeited; it cannot be lost; it cannot be altered; it cannot be suppressed."

The quest for physical law is a spiritual quest. The mathematics necessary to undertake this quest is the fruit of reason. Reason is the first step toward the recognition of the patterned universe and human mastery of its physical constituents. Reason in turn demands an objective and quantitative approach to understanding the universe. Experiment born of predictive mathematics is the divine conveyance by which the Creator affixes verifiable approval to our interpretations. No human institution can hide the length of the day or the position of the stars in the sky.

The physical laws discovered from the motion of the planets can be applied to the motion of blood in our veins or of water in the oceans or of hydrogen boiling deep inside a star. Because physical law applies uniformly to all constituents of the physical universe, it must ultimately impact our knowledge and understanding of ourselves: our societies, our bodies, our consciousness.

The discoveries of modern physical law have led to revelations about the nature of time and space, about the structure of reality itself, that are alien to everyday experience and expectation. No human mind could have conceived of the truths that were revealed in the mathematics. One strange discovery was that subatomic particles can move from point A to point B without necessarily traveling the intervening distance. Such a particle also may simultaneously travel along two different paths through space. These discoveries and many others like them will continue to profoundly alter both the course of human history and the evolution of human consciousness.

Paine could not have known how profound the path of the "true and fabulous theology" would be when he wrote:

> That which is now called natural philosophy, embracing the whole circle of science, of which Astronomy occupies the chief place, is the study of the works of God, and of the power and wisdom of God in his works, and is the true theology.[2]

When Paine wrote this in 1794, physical law consisted of little more than Newton's discoveries and Euclidean geometry.

The science of Paine's day was embryonic compared with science today. The revolutions in physical law since Newton have revealed a "true theology" that is spectacular and fantastic. Mathematics is somehow a bridge between the human mind and the mind of the Creator. Through mathematics we have deciphered the sacred text of physical law.

π and e are only the most common of a host of special numbers discovered in geometry and mathematics, numbers which find great utility in the description of physical law. But there is another special group of numbers which were discovered in the world around us. We do not know why they have their particular values, nor can we calculate them as we can for e. How accurately we know these numbers depends on our ability to measure them; it is unlikely we will ever be able to calculate them. These special numbers are *the physical constants*.

Unlike π and e, the physical constants have units. They are not dimensionless numbers. If you are weighed by a doctor in Europe, you will find that the number of your weight is different than when it is measured in America. This is not because your weight has changed, but because weight is measured in kilograms in Europe and pounds in America. Weight is an example of a number which depends on the units used to measure it.

Most numbers of interest have units. The age of a person (years) or the length of the day (hours) or the distance to the grocery store (miles). In the same way, the numerical values of the physical constants depend on the the units we choose to measure distance, time, electric charge, and mass.

Nevertheless, the physical constants were not written by man. They are so few and so profound as to mark the separate books of the bible of physical law. These books are numbered with G – the gravitational constant, $(4\pi\epsilon_0)^{-1}$ – the electric constant, c – the speed of light, H – the Hubble constant, and $\hbar$ – the Planck constant.

The discovery of each of the physical constants heralded a revolution in understanding. Each spawned dramatic technological and economical changes. Examples of such technologies include radio, nuclear energy, electrical power generation, and transistor chips. Such technologies were in turn based upon revolutionary concepts about the nature of the universe. These concepts include the equivalence of mass and energy, the existence of force fields, and the wave nature of matter.

The pursuit and development of science over the past few centuries has been a collective achievement. Thousands of scientists assembled bits of data and built progressively more sophisticated explanations for them. At certain times, the agglomeration of data outstripped the ability of the understanding of physical law to explain the measurements. These were times of transformation in human understanding. These were times of enlightenment, when a veil was pulled away to show the Creator's design at a more powerful and subtle level. At each of these thresholds of discovery a new physical constant was discovered and new mathematical physical laws were developed.

At each of these times a single individual appeared who catalyzed the transformation and who first made the leap of consciousness. These individuals were the first to hear the new mathematical Word of God and bring down from the mountain another book of knowledge. They are the prophets of the quest to read the Word in Creation. They are the archetypes of scientific discovery, the great masters of physical law. Their stories are the stepping stones to the emergence of consciousness as a factor in the mathematical formulation of physical law.

This magnificent journey of physical law began as an act of faith.

Faith

Before science there was faith. Over the past few centuries, science and religion have both pivoted on the fulcrum of faith. Faith is the necessary first element of science or religion. In religion, you must believe in the god you worship. In science, you must believe in the order you seek. Faith is a force that drove first religion then science. Physical law started with the physics of faith.

Mathematical physical law emerged in post-Renaissance Europe. The discoveries in physical law during this time were within a framework of Christian beliefs. This included seeking the glory of God in the perfect mathematical patterns characterizing the universe. While such efforts may have been opposed by the Christian clergy, scientists of many religious faiths over many generations have continued to see the patterned universe as an expression of God's greater glory.

Monotheism, the belief in a single god, formed the scaffolding of faith for the construction of physical law because it implied a single divine order. The details of Christian doctrine were not as important to the discovery of physical law as the broader notion of monotheism itself. Indeed, during the European Middle Ages, the light of reason was nurtured in the Islamic societies of the Middle East. But that turning point in human consciousness, the mathematical formulation of physical law, occurred in Christian Europe. The essential element for human conception of physical law was faith, faith in a single God, faith in a single divine plan. Early European explorations of the order underlying the world were to reveal the glory of God's handiwork, the divine plan and construction. The unity of monotheism was a necessary element in the evolution of human consciousness toward comprehension of physical law.

While they spring from the same ultimate source, the faith necessary for physical law is of a kind more sublime than the faith that drives belief in deities. It is faith in a dance coordinated among all creation that is not capricious, but preordained. Monotheism itself is not enough to sustain science. Science is sustained instead by a religious doctrine that can be called *omnitheism*, the belief that all parts of the universe obey the same governing laws. No bit of matter is immune. Everything is divine but nothing is special. The oxygen and carbon of our bodies would serve equally well in that of a king or a slave or a rock. The basis of mathematical physical law was a sort of religious omnitheism which implied faith in one universe, one set of principles guiding matter, all things for all time waltzing to the same divine music.

The first labor pang heralding the birth of mathematical physical law was the suggestion that perhaps humanity was not the center of the divine universe. Such notions ran counter to the tenets of medieval European Christianity. Instead, the Christian doctrine stated that humankind existed at the very center of the universe, that humankind was the whole purpose for the universe. The Polish astronomer Copernicus is credited with introducing, in 1543, the idea into Western thought that the earth was not at the center of the universe but instead moved around the sun.

Copernicus heralded not just a discovery, but a triumph. It was the triumph of reason over superstition. The other discoveries of physical law which followed in the centuries after Copernicus mark the first appearances of traits and truths that humanity is destined to adopt. At each such juncture of scientific history, the inescapable becomes accepted. Seen through the eye of reason, truth becomes inescapable. Because the truth is inescapable, superstition must succumb to the objective world.

The gradual acceptance of the Copernican idea expressed a certain maturation of humanity. It marked a point at which European society had matured enough to let go any need or desire to be at the center of creation. Although more ancient societies deduced the motion of the earth, this was lost in the West until Copernicus. This mature world view was a necessary first step along the road to a mathematical formulation of physical law and the true unlocking of the secrets of the universe. Free from superstition, we are able to discover the true underlying mathematical order of the universe.

It fell to the German astronomer Kepler (1571-1630) to discover the mathematical description of the planets' motion around the sun. Based on years of painstaking observations by his patron, Tycho, Kepler found planetary orbits were not circles, as envisioned by Copernicus, but neat mathematical figures called ellipses. He also found the planets sped up in their orbits near the sun, and slowed down moving farther away, always following a precise mathematical description.

Kepler's discoveries were an expression of the harmony and order of nature equal to the poetry of any culture, but now in the language of mathematics. Their explanation in terms of physical law would await Newton. But they mark the recognition of a mathematical order underlying the universe, of simple expressions governing colossal forces.

For many Europeans, Kepler's laws confirmed their belief in a divine order underlying the universe. They realized that for the universe to manifest such order as expressed in Kepler's laws, all parts of the universe must be obeying the same physical laws. All parts of the universe are under divine influence. This is the notion of *universal* physical law.

Universal physical law is simply the concept that all parts of the universe obey the same rules governing their physical evolution. It means assuming a hydrogen atom on earth obeys the same rules as one in the center of the sun. This idea of one universe and one traffic cop for physical law is a necessary precursor to the formulation of mathematical physical law. The inclination to believe in a universal order, to assume it at the outset as the only reasonable assumption, can only be called faith. It is similar to the faith that informs a belief in God, but it is the omnitheistic faith in a discoverable mathematical universe.

The life of Galileo (1564-1642) marked the dawn of universal physical law in Western thought. Galileo had undertaken various observations of the motion of thrown and falling objects and interpreted them within a framework of universal physical law. That is, he attempted to deduce the laws governing their behavior by taking measurements of their motion.

Galileo also pioneered what we now call *the scientific method* and codified it as the form of human dialog with Creation. The scientific method is built upon repeatable experiments. The scientific method is democratic in that no experimenter is special, which follows because of the universality of physical law. Anyone is able to perform the same experiment and achieve the same results. In this way nature's secrets are revealed, free from superstition and bias, open to all for verification.

Ironically, Galileo's quest to know the mind of God led him to become a martyr for science. He was condemned in 1633 by the Catholic Church for teaching the Copernican doctrine. Instead of allowing its dogma to evolve along with greater human understanding of the natural universe, the Church resisted change and sought instead to suppress the new realizations.

The result of setting itself apart from physical law was that the Church initiated the demise of its own political relevancy. When neolithic societies were faced with crisis, salvation was sought in the wise opinions of shamen, those who were considered in touch with the mysterious forces of nature. Their political authority derived from societal beliefs in gods and dieties and the belief that shamen were capable of interpreting, influencing, and predicting the whims of the gods. As the evolution of human spirituality slowly transformed shamen into priests and polytheism into monotheism, the political role of the shaman remained. In medieval Europe, the Christian Church played a strong role in politics and government. But today, when the world's democracies are faced with crisis, they turn not to clerics but to scientists.

That science should displace religion is natural. As our species evolves, our spiritual conceptions advance in subtlety *along with* our material conceptions. We have replaced the weather gods with the equations of fluid dynamics, but it is no less wonderful. Instead of the weather gods capriciously deciding at each instant what the weather will be the following instant, creation obeys a directive that is described at all times by the equations of fluid dynamics.

In terms of their practical roles in society, the scientist has displaced the medicine man, the astrologer, and the rainmaker.

But we have not lost spiritually. Indeed, exploration of physical law seems to lead us along a path of expanding consciousness, a path laid down for us to find. Once we start upon the road of repeatable experiment and objective measurement, it becomes impossible to turn from the truths discovered along the way.

While the Catholic Church originally resisted seeing the discovery of physical law as the discovery of divine order, the great discoverers of natural law from Copernicus to Einstein were all deeply religious. For them, their discoveries were in harmony with their religious beliefs. To them, their discoveries did not overturn religion but strengthened it, for they gave precise expression to the divine order of our universe. Revealing this order was *proof* of the divine. The discoveries to be made would constitute a growth and strengthening of human spiritual conviction. In their quest to find the author of π, they exercised their faith.

For teaching the Copernican doctrine, the Church placed Galileo under house arrest until his death in 1642. But the light of divine reason was not extinguished for, in that same year of 1642, Isaac Newton was born.

Force

There was no more profound moment in the history of life on earth than when Isaac Newton did proclaim:

> In the third Book I give an ... explication of the Systems of the World; for by the propositions mathematically demonstrated in the former Books, in the third I derive from the celestial phenomena the forces of gravity with which bodies tend to the sun and the several planets. Then from these forces, by other propositions which are also mathematical, I deduce the motions of the planets, the comets, the moon and the sea.[3]

Newton was the first, and the greatest, of the prophets of mathematical physical law. His revelation was the physics of force and of the mathematical forms used to describe physical law to this day. It was the discovery of a predictive understanding of nature, the first truly useful understanding of nature. It was when we began to reach for the stars.

This first book of physical law is numbered with *G*, the gravitational constant discovered by Newton. Although *G* was the first of the physical constants to be discovered, it remains among the most poorly known. Some of the physical constants are known to better than a part in 10 million, but *G* is known only to a part in ten thousand. Writing out π, for example, to a part in 10 million would be 3.141593. Knowing it to a part in ten thousand would simply be 3.142; this is how poorly we know the value of *G*.

The numerical value of *G* depends upon our choice to measure length in meters (m), mass in kilograms (kg), and time in seconds (s). It could just as easily be given in units of inches for length or hours for time, changing its numerical value from the standard value written in the header. Nonetheless, *G* is the signature of the author of gravity. It numbers the book of Force.

Newton's great achievement was to synthesize Galileo's work on the laws of motion with his own discovery of the law of gravity. He also created the mathematics necessary for the expression of both. He called this mathematics *fluxions*. We know it as *calculus*. Although it is but one branch of mathematics today, calculus is the language of physical law.

Calculus is the mathematics of change. It addresses quantities that change continually in time or space, like the position of a revolving planet or the flow of waves on an ocean. Although the concepts underlying physical law have changed much since Newton's time, the mathematical framework of using calculus to describe physical law remains virtually unchanged. Newton's fluxions continue to provide a mathematical framework for describing everything from black holes to quantum computers.

Newton compiled his many discoveries in his 1686 opus, *Mathematical Principles of Natural Philosophy*. It remains a blueprint for the formulation of physical law followed to this day. Although not the first scientist, Newton was the first physicist. But neither of those terms existed then. Newton was instead considered a scholar of "natural philosophy" and the first to apply mathematics to it. Written in Latin, Newton's work is usually referred to by its abbreviated title, *The Principia*. In it, Newton laid out discoveries of mathematical physical law that explained everything from the precession of the equinoxes to the trajectories of cannon balls. It was the motion of all things great and small, described by simple mathematical relations.

You don't need to be a physicist to play baseball but every ball player intuitively understands the concepts of mass and velocity. Everyone who has ever run or jumped or thrown a rock understands them. The key to physical law is to put a number on them, to *quantify* mass and velocity. Putting a number on the thrown rock is the first step to predicting where it will land, and that is nothing less than predicting the future.

The fundamental concepts that Newton discovered, necessary for predictive physical law, were *force* and *momentum.* Force and momentum are the yin and yang of motion. Momentum is a measure of motion, and force is the thing that, when applied, changes momentum. Changes in momentum come about through forces and no changes occur in the absence of forces. Every water molecule, baseball, or planet has a numerical value of momentum, calculated simply as the value of its mass multiplied by its velocity. A heavy object moving slowly can have the same momentum as a light object moving rapidly. A buzzing fly has more momentum than a battleship moored in port. Furthermore, force, velocity, and momentum are all mathematical quantities known as *vectors.*

Technically, a vector is just a set of three numbers. Vectors are mathematical quantities whose properties largely reflect the triple dimensionality of space. Because space is three-dimensional, to specify any position in space requires three numbers. The three numbers that specify that position form a vector. Which three numbers you use depends upon your *coordinate system,* the way in which you choose to measure things. However, the real position in space does not depend upon whether distance is measured in inches or meters. There is an essential reality that transcends our choice of references. It is the reality of three spatial dimensions.

Newton's problem was to explain motion and to predict motion. To do this he needed a mathematical *measure* of motion. Momentum is that measure. In fact, one can hardly imagine a simpler quantity to characterize how much a thrown baseball will hurt if it hits you. It is just the mass of a thing multiplied by its velocity. This accords with our intuition because it tells us the pain of impact increases with the speed of the ball or with an increase in its mass. With these simple yet precise definitions, the law of gravity predicts how the momentum of any baseball or planet changes under gravity's influence.

Here, then, was the first quantitative expression of the nature of our universe, the first mathematical physical law: Newton's law of gravity. It describes the numerical value of the gravitational force F between two bodies of mass m_1 and m_2 separated by a distance r:

$$F = G\frac{m_1 m_2}{r^2}$$

The numerical value of the gravitational force between any two bodies is proportional to the product of their two masses, divided by the square of the distance separating them. From this force we may deduce the change in momentum of the two bodies. The force is attractive between m_1 and m_2, drawing them together. The strength of the force is fixed by the number G, the gravitational constant. Newton's expression for gravity was the first fundamental force discovered in nature, and with it came the first numerical constant of nature. The number *G* is the fingerprint of gravity in our universe.

Applied to the planets, Newton's laws of gravity and motion explained Kepler's observations. When they are applied to the moon and oceans, the tides are explained. These same laws predict the ballistic behavior of projectiles and the engineering stresses of buildings. This is the meaning of universal physical law, that it applies to everything. The discovery of the laws of motion and gravity revealed a divine simplicity underlying our universe.

For two centuries after Newton, his equations were applied across a wide range of phenomena from planetary motion in our solar system to designing bicycles and airplanes. Even today, Newton's laws of motion and gravity are sufficiently precise to predict the complex trajectories of interplanetary spacecraft. When Newton's laws were formulated for fluids, the dynamics of wind and water were understood. Rigorous ideas about the relations between mass, momentum, force, and velocity became staples of the engineering disciplines. Various auxiliary forces were discovered: frictional force, centrifugal force, and viscous force. None of these latter forces is a truly fundamental force of nature like gravity but they demonstrate the widespread utility of the concept of force. The concept of force is the key element in the prediction and interpretation of physical phenomena.

During the centuries following Newton another essential concept was discovered: *energy*. Although not known to Newton, energy is a concept auxiliary to force and is perhaps more fundamental than force. A measure of energy is obtained by multiplying the numerical strength of a force with the distance over which the force is exerted. For example, the energy required to raise an object against the force of gravity is the distance raised multiplied by the object's weight.

Newton's laws tell us that for isolated systems of matter far from the influence of any forces, the total momentum and energy of the system are *conserved.* That is, momentum and energy remain constant in the system. These were the first *conservation principles*. As our understanding of physical law continued to develop over the centuries, conservation principles continued to be discovered for a variety of systems.

Of the several quantities that nature conserves, momentum and energy are particularly noteworthy. Their conservation reflects the fact that physical law does not change with time (conservation of energy) or through space (conservation of momentum). This is because if the laws of physics changed as one moved through space, a body could not move freely across such regions without feeling some sort of force which would divert its momentum. If the laws of physics changed with time, then a body could not exist in time without experiencing a change in its energy content.

With such simple concepts as energy and momentum, Newtonian physical law can be recast entirely in terms of conservation principles. It is fantastic that the very form of physical law can be derived mathematically by merely assuming the laws of physics don't vary with space or time. Such sublime simplicity presages Einstein's discoveries.

In addition to his numerous scientific precedents, Newton set a sociological one: many of the greatest discoveries of physical law are made by people in their early 20's. Newton's revelations were received by age 24. Those rare flashes of brilliance that manifest suddenly in the minds of a select few, and change forever human conception of physical reality, tend to favor the young. As the reader will later see, this sociological fact will have profound consequences for the course of science during the discovery and understanding of the pilot wave.

Although he made great discoveries as a young man, Newton did not reveal them to the world until 20 years later, with publication of the *Principia.* During those intervening years, the German mathematician Leibniz independently discovered the calculus and established the modern notation for it. Although the most advanced scientific mind on the planet, Newton was not similarly advanced emotionally. He indulged himself in a vengeful crusade against Leibniz to establish his primacy of discovery and used his influence in an attempt to destroy Leibniz's career. This, too, would turn out to be another sociological precedent: the stately ship of science rocked by inevitable waves of human frailty.

This illustrates one way in which the omnitheism of

physical law differs from the monotheism of some religions: the prophets of physical law espouse a verifiable truth. The truths of the text-based religions of faith follow from the presumed divinity of their priesthoods. When a member of such a preisthood causes harm to one of the faithful, or causes harm to the trust of the faithful, then the truths of the priest may be questioned. Why would God choose a flawed vessel to carry the message? The truths of prophets such as Newton are self-evident. The moral frailty of such prophets does not endanger the divinity of their message. In our quest to know the author of π, morality is not an element. The truth of what Newton discovered is independent of his morality.

In the Age of Reason, human frailty could do nothing to undermine the truth Newton discovered. Newton's access to the divine inhabited the realm of the objective and whatever his weakness of morals or ethics, his discoveries of the mathematical Word of the Creator are beyond dispute. Newton was a mere mortal, yet he approached the godhead. He possessed that perfect pitch which allowed us to begin to transcribe the music of the spheres. Now the myriad patterns of matter weaving our world can be understood as the manifestation of simple mathematical expressions, expressions simple enough even for humans to understand. We have only to put pencil to paper to compute, predict, and *know*.

For Newton and other men of faith who made subsequent discoveries of physical law, mathematics was the language of the universe, the language of God. Newton showed us that physical law is a bible written across all creation. Its revelation requires neither priest nor prophet, but instead *measurement*.

Yet questions remained in Newton's wake. How do forces act? By what means does the sun tug on the earth via gravity? How does gravity grab a thing? Newton could not answer these questions. For Newton and for many that followed, gravity was a mysterious "action-at-a-distance." There was some connection between objects separated in space but insight into the nature of that connection would await Einstein. Newton's vision of physical law would, however, stand pristine for two centuries before the next great insight into the nature of reality: *fields* of force.

Field

You are an electromagnetic being. You live in an electromagnetic world. All you see, feel, and hear are electromagnetic phenomena. The atoms and molecules in your body are bound together by electromagnetic forces. Everything experienced by any creature on earth is an electromagnetic experience. The electromagnetic *field* is the underpinning of reality as we know it.

As fundamental as electromagnetism is to our material existence, so was it fundamental to our conception of natural law. It was when the physics of force was overtaken by the physics of field. The field concept was a subtle refinement of the concept of force. Force is what is measurable, but the field provides the force. The concept of the force field emerged as a mathematical artifice, a way of expressing a measurable force. Now it is accepted that it is the field which is fundamental.

Forces are waves upon the ocean; field is the ocean itself. Our prophet of the field was James Clerk Maxwell. The book of knowledge he brought down from the mountain is numbered with $(4\pi\epsilon_0)^{-1}$.

In the 18th and early 19th centuries, experiments revealed forces separate from gravity. These forces involved electricity and magnetism. The phenomenon of magnetism had been known throughout human history. It had been seen in rocks and metals, used in compasses. The phenomenon of electricity is also widespread in nature. Its dramatic power is seen in lightning. We experience it directly through the shock of static electricity or see its flashes of light merely by peeling off a sweater. By the mid-19th century, a large body of information existed concerning the electric and magnetic forces. The mathematical simplicity seen in gravity was also reflected in measurements of electrical and magnetic phenomena.

There is a property of matter which controls how strongly a body is influenced by the electric force. This property is called *electric charge* and is completely analogous to the role played by mass in Newton's law of the gravitational force. Unlike mass, however, there are two types of charge: positive and negative. The two types express the possibility for either attraction or repulsion between two charged objects. The mathematical expression for the electric force between two charged objects was established in the late 18th century and is named after its discoverer, Charles de Coulomb:

$$F=(4\pi\epsilon_0)^{-1}\frac{Q_1 Q_2}{r^2} \quad .$$

Remarkably, the electric force and the gravitational force have the same mathematical form, with mass (m) and charge (Q) playing analogous roles. One calculates from this expression the change of momentum imparted to bodies of charge Q_1 and Q_2 separated by a distance r . There exists an electrical constant $(4\pi\epsilon_0)^{-1}$ which, like G, is a fixed property of our universe. This constant quantifies the strength of the electric force just as G quantifies the strength of the gravitational force. The electrical force constant is written in a complicated way for historical reasons.

As for G, the numerical value of the electric constant depends on the units we choose to measure mass, distance, and time. It also depends on our choice of unit for electric charge, the Coulomb (C). Charge and mass play analogous roles in the electrical and gravitational force laws. The coulomb is a unit of charge just as the kilogram is a unit of mass. The constant which calibrates the strength of the electric force in our universe, ϵ_0, is formally known as the *permittivity of free space*. Unlike the gravitational constant, $(4\pi\epsilon_0)^{-1}$ is known precisely and the value written in the header is exact. The coulomb was already defined in terms of a unit of electric current, the ampere. Because units are then already defined for force, charge, and distance, there is no freedom in the electrical constant. Its value can be stated exactly because of choices made with respect to the definition of the units of charge, distance, mass, and time.

It is not a big conceptual step to go from Newton's law of gravity to Coulomb's law but it nonetheless was the first step toward the revolutionary concept of the force field.

Seemingly separate from the electric force, it was well-known that a magnetic force existed which would turn a bar magnet to point along a magnetic north-south line. Two magnets placed near each other tend to repel or attract one another, depending on their relative orientation. Surprisingly, experiments revealed that forces existed between two wires carrying electric current just like the forces between two magnets. Electric currents generate magnetic forces!

Andre Marie Ampere mathematically described the strength of the magnetic force accompanying a wire carrying electric current. His magnetic experiments revealed there was a magnetic constant just as there was an electrical constant and a gravitational constant. This magnetic constant is now typically written μ_0 and is known as the *permeability of free space*. It is completely analogous to ϵ_0 and together they are the two fundamental constants of electromagnetism. The force law for magnetism, however, does not share the classic r^{-2} form seen in both the gravitational and electrical force laws.

The discovery of electric and magnetic forces, and their respective mathematical expressions and numerical constants, was a triumph of Newton's legacy of quantitative interpretation of nature. But the wonder of the electric and magnetic forces did not stop there. Michael Faraday discovered an electric force accompanies a changing magnetic force. If a bar magnetic were moved through a wire loop, for example, an electric current would arise in the loop. So, not only do electric currents create magnetic forces, but magnetic forces also create electric currents.

The discoveries regarding the electric and magnetic forces of Coulomb, Ampere, and Faraday still fit within Newton's framework. It seemed there were going to be many forces in nature, each with a simple mathematical formula and an accompanying constant of nature. But these discoveries were mere prelude to the next great conceptual landmark of human understanding of physical law: the electromagnetic field. The name associated with this revolution in understanding is that of the Scotsman James Clerk Maxwell.

During the mid-1800s, Maxwell was a prodigy in the practice of an art which had remained quite similar to what Newton would have called natural philosophy. Calculus was well established but there were basic discoveries in physics yet to come. Many scientists were gentlemen amateurs of means and curiosity. The world's most advanced experimental apparatus might be in someone's home. It was a fertile time for all of science. Topics of debate included the most efficient notation for calculus, the implications of Darwin's theory of evolution for both Christianity and the age of the earth, whether matter consisted of atoms or was infinitely divisible, and even the origin of the force of gravity.

Maxwell was born of landed gentry, a man of independent means with time enough for scholarly pursuits. But he was also a country boy. The countryside of his rural estate was his playground and an infinite field for exploration. His father was scientifically inclined and took the young Maxwell on outings to factories and farms to show his son how things worked. The boy's curiosity was apparent early on. His mother's journals show that at age two, “He has great work with doors, locks, keys, etc and 'Show me how it doos' is never out of his mouth.”[4]

Only his contributions to electromagnetism are being discussed here, but Maxwell made numerous contributions to our understanding of the physical universe. He revolutionized the related branches of science known as thermodynamics, kinetic theory, and statistical mechanics. Like Newton, he had a keen interest in optics and proved that human eyes have three kinds of color receptors: red, blue, and green. He was able to prove the rings of Saturn were made of small particles, and contributed foundational discoveries to the mathematical field of topology. Like many of the great physicists, he was an impeccable experimentalist. He was able to prove to himself by direct measurement many of his theoretical discoveries. Such self-verified discoveries include the viscosity of air and the speed of light.

For his electrical work, Maxwell stood on the shoulders of giants, particularly Faraday. It was Faraday who first developed ideas which would be a stepping stone to the field concept. Faraday had an irrational fear of mathematics which perhaps forced him to develop a strong intuitive grasp of physical law. He used his discoveries to build a physical picture of electric and magnetic forces and went on to develop the concept of magnetic lines of force. These lines of force can be traced out in a classic demonstration involving a magnet placed below a paper on which are sprinkled iron filings. The small magnetic whiskers will line up and point along the lines of force, resembling the pattern revealed when slicing an onion in half.

Like Faraday, Maxwell also had a genius for visual thinking. While many scientists were skeptical of attempts to construct a physical picture of electromagnetic phenomena, Maxwell cottoned to Faraday's ideas. In fact, Maxwell developed a new mathematical formalism to describe Faraday's discoveries, a feat which left Faraday in awe and gratitude.

The basic elements of modern calculus are the complementary concepts of the integral and the differential. The integral tells us about quantities added up over all space. The differential tells us how quantities change in each bit of space and time. As many of the mathematical expressions of electric and magnetic forces used an integral formalism, a large part of Maxwell's systemization was to show how the laws of electricity and magnetism could be described in terms of differential calculus. The differential formalism would be necessary for Maxwell's triumphal discovery of wave solutions to the combined equations of electricity and magnetism.

Maxwell made a major practical contribution to science by bringing order to the anarchic set of units used to measure electrical and magnetic effects. He rationalized them with the familiar units of length, time, and mass used in Newtonian physical law. This rationalization of units ultimately lead to the value of the electric constant written in the header above.

Before he accomplished the mathematical triumph we remember to this day, Maxwell constructed a model of electricity and magnetism based on mechanical concepts of microscopic gears spanning all space. With his clockwork model of electricity and magnetism, he was able to derive all the exceptional and remarkable results he later obtained through mathematics. When he finally got to the mathematics, he already knew which solutions to look for. Maxwell was, in fact, known for the frequency of mathematical and even conceptual errors in his scientific papers. Yet his visual genius allowed him to unerringly find the right answer, even if he couldn't always prove it.

His treatise on electromagnetism, written late in his life, was his proudest achievement and scarce of any sort of error. It was the culmination of two decades of work. Maxwell's genius seemed only to grow with time and had he not died of stomach cancer at the age of 48, it is speculated he would have discovered the electron.

What he did do was show how rich diversity can arise from divine simplicity. Maxwell recognized that the separate force laws of electricity and magnetism could be understood as different expressions of a single fundamental force. The mathematical key to this unification was for him to suppose that changing electric forces should generate magnetic forces to mirror Faraday's discovery that changing magnetic forces generated electric forces. Accounting for this effect mathematically had the advantage of making the combined set of electric and magnetic equations conserve electric charge; electric charge is neither created nor destroyed. Although a supposition at the time, conservation of electric charge has endured as a pillar of physical law alongside conservation of energy and momentum.

Maxwell's addition to the mathematical laws of electricity and magnetism created a wonderful symmetry: changing magnetic forces inevitably create electric forces, and changing electric forces inevitably create magnetic forces. The electric and magnetic forces were discovered separately and they seem unrelated. Yet these forces are apparently different aspects of the same physical phenomenon. If one is altered the other is created. This duality is the idea behind the term *electromagnetic.*

Controlling these forces would turn out to be quite useful for humanity. Spinning magnets create electric currents in everything from hydroelectric dams to automobile alternators. Electric motors then convert the electricity into useful work by inverting the process: the magnetic field accompanying a changing electric current will spin a magnet attached to a drive shaft. But that useful application of Maxwell's electromagnetism, the large scale generation of electric power, would await the work of Nicola Tesla late in the 19th century.

The stamp of divine approval on Maxwell's modification of the laws of electricity and magnetism was that the full set of combined equations supported solutions representing traveling waves. Just like the waves one might see on the surface of a pond, there can be waves in the electric and magnetic forces. A stationary observer would see an electric wave as a sudden increase in the local strength of the electric force and then a return to normal values as the wave went by. The nature of these electromagnetic waves involves both electric and magnetic forces which oscillate back and forth as the wave travels. The stationary observer might see a fluctuation in the electric force and then an instant later a fluctuation in the magnetic force.

The speed at which these waves travel was found to be a constant independent of the frequency of the wave. This constant is given in terms of our friends μ_0 and ϵ_0, who together specify the magnetic and electric constants. This wave speed is, in fact, *the speed of light*. It is known fondly to scientists everywhere as c.

When Maxwell showed that light is an electromagnetic wave, he unified into a single coherent whole an extraordinary diversity of physical phenomena. The spectrum of electromagnetic radiation includes radio waves, microwaves, infrared radiation, visible light, ultraviolet light, X-rays, and gamma rays. Many of these manifestations were unknown to Maxwell, an indication of the power of the mathematical framework he discovered. The elegant beauty of Maxwell's discovery was of a historical primacy which caused the laws of Coulomb, Ampere, and Faraday to be seen as different parts of a set of equations known ever after as the Maxwell equations.

The speed of light c is so large that it was difficult to measure directly in the time of Maxwell. So, for many years, the best estimate of its value was calculated from laboratory measurements of μ_0 and ϵ_0. Such measurements are typically undertaken with relatively primitive apparatus. To be able to determine c based on lab experiments with objects such as electrically-charged pith balls and small electric circuits, experiments that seem quite unrelated to the propagation of light, was an amazing testament to the growing depth and subtlety of human understanding of physical law. It revealed a fundamental unity of nature and reaffirmed the predictive power obtained by making careful measurements of seemingly disparate phenomena.

Maxwell maintained unshakable Christian beliefs his entire

life, even as the truths of the age of the earth and the evolution of species emerged during his life time. But his discoveries were inseparable from his deity, as on his deathbed he said,

> What is done by what is called myself is, I feel, done by something greater than myself in me.[5]

He indeed connected his faith with his science, as when he said:

> As Physical Science advances we see more and more that the laws of nature are not mere arbitrary and unconnected decisions of Omnipotence, but that they are essential parts of one universal system in which infinite Power serves only to reveal unsearchable Wisdom and eternal Truth....Is it not wonderful that man's reason should be made a judge over God's works, and should measure, and weigh, and calculate, and say at last "I understand I have discovered -- It is right and true"?[6]

The discoveries of one of the greatest prophets of physical law lived harmoniously under his roof with a Christian spiritual tradition. As for many others before and after him, Maxwell's discoveries revealed a divine order which complemented his spiritual beliefs. He harbored no doubt that the Creator intended we find these patterns in the strata of physical reality.

Although Maxwell did not realize it, the electromagnetic force concept gave way in the subsequent decades to a concept which, in hindsight, seems inescapable: the electromagnetic field. This concept, implied all along in the Maxwell equations, was a revolution in physical understanding. The field exists everywhere in the universe and it is the electric and magnetic forces which are transient. Those forces spring from their source in the field and return to it.

We describe the shape of this field with the electric and magnetic force vectors, which can, in principle, be measured at any place or time. Every force vector is characterized by a strength and a direction, and those of the electric and magnetic force vectors provide a complete mathematical specification of the electromagnetic field.

How is the concept of a force field so different from just force? Why is the field concept necessary? To answer these questions, we must go back to Newton's law of gravity. That law quantitatively described a force of attraction between any two massive objects. But how was the force communicated? How is it that the sun exerts a gravitational force on the earth, or the earth on the moon? Newton's law of gravity doesn't tell us how gravity acts, only its strength.

Newton realized that his law of gravity implied “action at a distance”. No matter how widely separated two objects are, the force of gravity exists. There was no outrunning the force of gravity. If you magically created a massive object anywhere in the universe, it would, according to Newton's law of gravity, be instantly under the influence of the cumulative gravitational force of all other massive objects in the universe. There would be no delay for the force of gravity to reach it and no delay for it to influence everything else in the universe. According to Newton's law, mere existence was the only prerequisite for full and instantaneous participation in gravitation.

This is why Faraday's idea of lines of force was important to Maxwell. The lines of force promised the discovery of some mechanism by which the electric and magnetic forces exerted their influence, so that action at a distance could be avoided in electromagnetism. Knowing that his law of gravity implied action at a distance was a bit unsettling for Newton, but there was no arguing with the law's many successes. With electromagnetism, on the other hand, the field concept allowed escape from action at a distance. The concept of the field and its lines of force allowed physical law to approach an understanding of the mechanism by which forces act which was not available in Newton's laws.

Maxwell's laws of the electromagnetic force are much more complicated than Newton's law of the gravitational force. Where Newtonian gravity is described by one number at each point in space, electromagnetism requires four. Another difference is that identifying sources of electromagnetic forces can become intractable. This is particularly so because of electromagnetic waves. Electromagnetic waves propagate freely through space, altering the local electric and magnetic force vectors as they travel, existing independent of their sources. If you shine your flashlight into the sky, for example, the beam continues to travel long after you turn the light off. The electromagnetic force at any point is like the surface of the ocean, perpetually fluctuating and changing. It is impossible to identify all the flashlights sloshing the ocean. Once the light is created, its fate is entirely decoupled from that of its source.

The electric or magnetic forces can be anywhere zero at one instant, and assume large values the next instant. An electrically-charged particle is constantly sloshed about in this electromagnetic ocean in a way that does not happen with Newtonian gravity. This electromagnetic ocean of force is, of course, the electromagnetic field. It is enormously more complicated than the staid forces of Newtonian gravity, which are more akin to the frozen surface of a pond than the turbulent surface of an ocean.

Before Maxwell, the only question to ask concerning the dynamics of material objects was: Is there a force present? If there was no force of gravity, there was no gravity, period. But this picture does not hold with electromagnetic phenomena. If there is no electric force, we just say the value of the electric field happens to be zero. But we know it can, and will, change soon. There may even be a magnetic force if there is no electric force present.

It is the omnipresent electromagnetic field which is the essential reality. The value of its associated electric or magnetic force at any one time and at any one place is auxiliary and transitory. The field that supports traveling electromagnetic waves is a real entity, just as the surface of a pond supports waves from a stone long after the stone has dropped to the bottom. This is quite unlike Newtonian gravity, which states that if you magically removed any object from existence its contribution to the gravitational force would vanish as well.

Action at a distance does not appear in electromagnetism. The field is the medium by which electric and magnetic forces exert their pushes and pulls. Disturbances in this medium travel through it at the speed of light and no faster. For a charged object magically dropped into the universe, its influence would travel outward through the electromagnetic field at the speed of light, and the rest of the universe wouldn't know about the appearance of the object until the electromagnetic wave arrived.

Extrapolating the concept of the electromagnetic field to Newton's law of gravity, one can think of the force of gravity in terms of a gravitational field. Just as the electric field dictates the motion of all electrically-charged objects in the universe, so does the gravitational field control the motion of all objects with mass. Thus, electromagnetism brought about a retroactive refinement of notions about gravity. Unlike electromagnetism, however, there was no dynamics to the gravitational field. Newton's law of gravity involved no time dependence, and there was no magnetic counterpart to the gravity force, as there was to the electric force. There were apparently no Newtonian gravity waves.

It is remarkable that Newton's stepping stone would lead us to such revolutionary concepts. By trying to extend Newtonian-style laws to electric phenomena, lured with the baby step of Coulomb's law so seductively similar to Newton's law of gravity, humanity is brought face to face with the existence of a universal field of force. It exists everywhere in the universe, and we now know the experiences of living creatures are mere manifestations of its interplay. This is because the atoms in our bodies and in all terrestrial matter are bound together by electromagnetic forces. Chemistry is an electromagnetic phenomenon.

To go from the idea of mysterious yet quantitatively-known forces to the idea of a universally existing force field, real even in the absence of forces, is transcendent. We move from Newton's picture of objects in space and time bound by forces to a picture of reality as having an underlying fabric, the electromagnetic field. All our experiences and much of the material world is seen as a never-ending dance upon the infinite ocean of electromagnetism.

The field concept has far reaching implications for any spiritual doctrine which accommodates what is known about the universe. In the time of Newton and before, the universe seemed to operate as a divine mechanism, like pieces moving under computer control over a grand chess board. Things moved in space and interacted with one another according to known force laws. A spiritual doctrine tuned to this reality may envision a chess master overseeing the game.

In the age of the field, however, electromagnetic forces are mere manifestations of a greater plane of physical reality, the electromagnetic field. This field is a layer in the fabric of the universe itself. It is one of only a few such layers through which our universe expresses change and diversity. The forces binding the molecules in our bodies and underlying all of chemistry ultimately arise from the electromagnetic field. The forces binding the matter in our world and shaping the reality of our existence are tied inextricably to a greater ground of existence.

Electromagnetism taught us that fields of force exist in our universe, that light is electromagnetic in nature. It gave us the understanding required to develop the technological foundations of modern society. But it also harbored one further jewel for humanity. In the latter part of the 19th century, a young boy started to dream about what it would be like to surf on a wave of light. This electromagnetic dream led Albert Einstein to discover the geometry of space and time.

$$\nabla \times \boldsymbol{B} = \mu_0 \epsilon_0 \frac{\partial \boldsymbol{E}}{\partial t} + \mu_0 \boldsymbol{J} \qquad \nabla \cdot \boldsymbol{B} = 0$$

$$\nabla \times \boldsymbol{E} = -\frac{\partial \boldsymbol{B}}{\partial t} \qquad \nabla \cdot \boldsymbol{E} = \frac{\rho}{\epsilon_0}$$

Spacetime

One of the most magnificent journeys of intellectual discovery ever undertaken by an individual began from a Swiss patent office. From that office in the "miracle year" of 1905, at age 25, Albert Einstein submitted to an unbelieving world six scientific papers of monumental importance to science and physical law. Three were fundamental to the twin revolutions of 20th century physics: relativity and quantum theory. Had Einstein not done any work in the area of relativity, he would still be remembered as a giant of physics for his work on the quantum theory. Indeed, his Nobel prize did not mention relativity.

But Einstein also, single-handedly over the course of ten years, formulated the theory of relativity. Anyone believing in an objective reality which transcends the existence of any particular person must affirm that, had Einstein never lived, someone else would have discovered relativity. Perhaps this discovery would have occurred in a rapid succession of steps from among a small group of independent scientists, as happened with the quantum theory. The theory of relativity is, after all, merely an expression of the nature of physical reality. Yet it's uncanny that the whole thing should be the work of a single individual. The sense of awe for Einstein's feat is expressed in a quote attributed to his colleague, Arnold Sommerfeld:

> With profundity of thought and logicality of philosophical reasoning never before known in the mind of a natural scientist, and with mathematical power reminiscent of Gauss and Riemann, Einstein raised in the course of 10 years an edifice before which we who follow with rapt attention his labours from year to year must stand in amazement and stupor.[7]

The book of knowledge which Einstein brought down from the mountain is numbered with *c*, the speed of light. Although *c* was first quantified by Maxwell, it was first understood by Einstein. Light has the speed it does because of properties of our universe which transcend electromagnetism. The speed of light quantifies the relation of distance to time and of mass to energy. The value of *c* written above is exact because *c* is now used to define the meter (m) in terms of the second (s), so that the length of the meter is specified by how far a light wave travels in a certain fraction of a second. The speed of light could have been called the *Einstein constant*.

The theory of relativity stands as a unique conceptual landmark on the road to physical understanding. Unlike the advances in gravity and electromagnetism, there is no relativity force field. Rather, relativity dictates the form of any equation of physical law describing how objects move under the influence of forces. It does not matter whether the force is electric, gravitational, or anything else. Relativity applies to those forces discovered already and those yet to be discovered.

With the theory of relativity, deep understanding of nature was achieved by considering that physical law must abide a principle unrelated to any particular force or force field. This principle is the deceptively simple proposition that the laws of physics must be independent of your state of motion. This means that for scientists riding in spaceships at half the speed of light, for scientists in laboratories fixed to the surface of the revolving earth, for scientists playfully spinning on merry-go-rounds, the mathematical expressions of physical law are the same.

The field we call gravity was discovered by Einstein to have the unique property that its mathematical form is unchanged among all possible states of motion. The implication of Einstein's new mathematical form for gravity was to extend Newtonian gravity to a dynamical theory similar to Maxwell's equations of the dynamics of the electromagnetic field, but far more complex. It was ultimately a recognition that all things exist in space and time, and that our universe constrains their space and time aspects in certain ways.

How could such a discovery come about? It was pointed to by Maxwell's unified theory of electricity and magnetism, electrodynamics. Unknown to Maxwell, his electrodynamics was the first relativistically correct formulation of physical law. While Einstein completely reformulated Newtonian gravity and mechanics, electrodynamics remained untouched. In fact,

Einstein's founding paper from 1905 was titled, *On the electrodynamics of moving bodies*.

The key to relativity lies within the *coordinate systems,* the frameworks for numbering points in space and time, in which our expressions of physical law are embedded. Up through the time of Maxwell, every point in space was conveniently labeled within some *absolute* coordinate system. It was absolute in the sense that it was valid for any state of motion. For example, the coordinate system of latitude, longitude, and elevation is convenient for measuring positions near the surface of the earth. But since the earth is perennially swinging around the sun through space, our latitudes, longitudes, and elevations are really only useful for someone who happens to be fixed to the surface of the moving earth. A hypothetical Martian might do his measuring with respect to another coordinate system, a coordinate system convenient for him in which he is at rest and in which the earth happens to be moving. Our Martian may choose a coordinate system centered on the planet Mars, for example, or centered on the Sun.

All sets of coordinates are valid in that nature lets you

choose your coordinate system freely. The laws of physics don't demand we make our measurements in only certain coordinate systems any more than one could demand humans communicate in only a single language. But to practice physics at all requires a choice of some coordinate system, a system with which we can order quantitative measurements. We must make some choice of coordinates in which to make measurements before we can begin to undertake scientific study and measurement of the material world.

Our expressions of physical law must take proper account of the fact that they can be expressed in different coordinate systems, with these coordinate systems in motion *relative* to each other. This is where we actually get the name *relativity*. Scientists are free to formulate physical law in any coordinate system. Measurements can be made and the future behavior of a physical system can be predicted independent of the choice of coordinates. As Martians whiz by a naval exercise in their UFO, they are as able to measure the motion of an artillery shell and use the laws of physics to predict its impact point as are the sailors on the ship that fired it. If this were not so, there would be no objective physical reality.

Yet some things we measure do depend on our state of motion. One example is speed. A man on a platform sees a train go by and therefore he sees passengers moving with the speed of the train. But to a passenger on the train, the platform and the man standing on it appear to be moving. A man on the train is free to choose a coordinate system convenient for him, in which he is at rest, in which to make measurements. Some of the things that are useful to measure do depend on the state of motion they are measured from.

Even though the man on the train and the man on the platform may disagree on who is moving, there is a greater objective reality in which they both exist. There are certain aspects of the objective reality that cannot be changed by motion. If the man on the platform is reading the paper, the man on the train is not going to see him juggling balls, for example, or playing the violin, or see not a man at all but a zebra instead. Somehow the laws of physics must allow for these different states of motion and still describe the underlying reality faithfully. Yet some things will look different for the two men, depending on their states of relative motion. The theory of relativity shows us how to walk this fine line between what depends on your state of motion and what does not.

What was suggested by the Maxwell equations, and what Einstein discovered, is that space and time are bound by some odd relationships in our universe. These relationships may cause observers in different states of motion to disagree about their measurements of length and time. These relationships lead to the bizarre effects known as time dilation and length contraction. They also provide the famous link between mass and energy. Your conception of time and distance, relative to others, depends upon your motion relative to them.

A mathematical description of things living in space and time and which captures the essence of the objective reality requires a mathematical quantity that encompasses both space and time. Such a mathematical quantity is provided by the *4-vector.*

Newton revealed that some important elements of physical law, such as force, velocity, or momentum, have the mathematical properties of vectors. It takes three numbers to specify a vector because things described by vectors exist in space, and space is three-dimensional. The three dimensions correspond to the three distinct possibilities of motion apparent to an astronaut floating in space, or to a scuba diver under water: left-right, forward-backward, and up-down.

A 4-vector, on the other hand, has one time component and 3 space components. It is an ordinary 3-vector with an extra number for time. For example, a car crash can be described with a 4-vector because it has both an instant of time and a position in space associated with it. Things exist in time as well as space and we cannot ignore that in our understanding of physical law.

It is also true that for a 3-vector, its length and direction cannot depend on the coordinate system. This is because the underlying objective reality cannot depend on the coordinate system. If I determine that a comet is moving with a velocity vector directed toward the sun, for example, no one can come up with a coordinate system that has the comet going away from the sun. This is because a comet is a citizen of a greater objective reality which admits no fundamental contradictions.

If so, then whether the comet would hit the sun depends on an arbitrary choice of coordinates made by humans. Objective reality cannot work that way.

There is a fundamental reality represented by a 3-vector which transcends the human choice of coordinates. We call this reality the *geometry of space.* It is the physical reality of all things that exist in three spatial dimensions. Similarly, allowing that objects exist in both space and time, there is a *geometry of spacetime*.

It turns out that the geometry of spacetime in our universe is such that the length of a 4-vector has a numerical value that is the same measured from all states of motion and in all coordinate systems. While the length of a 3-vector depends on the state of motion from which it is measured, the length of the 4-vector does not. This mathematical conservation-of-length property is a fundamental expression of the geometry of spacetime, how space and time are related.

This thing we call the "length" of the 4-vector, however, is not at all intuitive. In the three-dimensional space that we are familiar with, the length of a vector is calculated as the sum of its three spatial components. In spacetime, the length of a 4-vector is the *difference* of its space and time components. The speed of light is used to convert the space and time components of the 4-vector to the same units, so that intervals of time can be sensibly subtracted from spatial distances. The numerical value of the speed of light is used to convert the time part of the 4-vector to space units or the space part of the 4-vector to time units. Nature doesn't care which units are chosen, demanding only that we properly convert between space and time units of measurement in calculating the lengths of 4-vectors. The value of c written above tells us that there are 299792458 meters of spatial distance in each second of elapsed time.

This conversion between the units of time and distance is where c enters as a fundamental constant in terms of the geometry of spacetime. Space and time do not have absolute fixed values in our universe but depend instead on the state of motion in which they are measured. Contrary to our separate notions of space and time, we learn they are actually parts of a single entity: spacetime. Spacetime is the reality, and its individual components are, to quote Einstein, "modes by which we think."

Einstein was not concerned with geometry, though. That was a subtle interpretation developed later by others. Einstein actually derived his theory of relativity from two assumptions. One was that the laws of physics were the same everywhere in space and time, in all states of motion. The second was that the speed of light is the same in all states of motion, even motion at the speed of light! That second assumption is perhaps the real expression of his genius.

The lore is that Einstein came upon the realization that the speed of light was the same in all states of motion by trying to imagine what it would be like to surf on a wave of light. He realized that light can never appear to be at rest with respect to any surfer, so that light must travel at the same speed independent of the state of motion.

The ghost of Copernicus haunts Einstein's hypothesis that the laws of physics are the same in all states of motion. Accepting that the universe favors no state of motion leads to the profound quantitative understanding of spacetime. It is equivalent in spirit to gaining understanding of the motion of the planets by letting go the desire to have earth be stationary and at the center of the universe. When we humble ourselves to the universe, when we seek universality and oneness in all phenomena, we are rewarded with understanding. This theme appears again and again in physical law.

Two stunning aspects of the nature of spacetime are that moving clocks run slower and moving yardsticks get shorter, as seen by someone watching them move. These effects are known respectively as *time dilation* and *length contraction*. Yardsticks measure only length and clocks measure only time, yet length and time are inseparable parts of the objective reality of spacetime. The slowing of moving clocks and the contraction of moving yardsticks are complementary expressions of the same physical reality. Only when these two elements are seen as constituents of a greater whole can the unchanging reality of spacetime be perceived.

The effect of time dilation causes astronauts, or even frequent fliers, to age slower than their earthbound brothers and sisters. These effects are not illusions. Time itself does actually slow down. But the astronaut notices nothing. Time goes by for her as it always has. She cannot detect that her clocks are running slower until she stops to compare them with a stationary clock. Such an astronaut would experience the same lifespan as an identical twin sister that never left the earth. It's just that the stationary twin would notice more than a year between the birthdays of her high flying sister. The flow of time appears to change relative to the state of motion, yet seems the same within every state of motion.

This means the state of one's motion can not be inferred from the flow of time within that state of motion. In the same way that an understanding of physical law proceeded from the Copernican realization that there is no special place in the universe, so was understanding gained by recognizing that there is no special state of motion.

Just as length and time are complementary aspects of an underlying objective reality, so are momentum and energy. Just as position and time comprise a 4-vector, so do momentum and energy. Any object moving in space and existing in time will have momentum and energy. The momentum and energy of a speeding train, for example, are obvious and intuitive. A speeding train, its huge iron mass proceeding along the track, is the epitome of momentum. The energy of its motion can be released in the destruction of a train wreck, or transformed into heat in its braking mechanism. Energy and momentum are both fundamental aspects of an object in motion.

Momentum and energy have different units, differing by a factor of distance divided by time. To combine them mathematically in a 4-vector requires just such a factor to be multiplied by one or the other. The speed of light provides just this factor. The special number c allows a time and a distance, or an energy and a momentum, to be mathematically united in 4-vectors.

With the unification of energy and momentum as complementary aspects of the underlying reality of an object in motion, Einstein reformulated their mathematical expressions which were originally discovered by Newton. He found that Newton's expressions were actually approximations valid for objects moving at speeds much less than c. Because c is so large, over 180,000 miles per second, the approximate nature of Newton's laws went undiscovered for centuries.

With energy and momentum seen to be complementary aspects of a more fundamental reality, the stage was set for another shattering realization: mass is bound energy. As may be expected for something which is bound, there is the implication that it may be released. The enormous energy released in nuclear weapons arises from the conversion of mass into energy. The stars in the sky shine by a conversion of mass to energy which is unrelenting over billions of years, while hardly reducing their mass in any appreciable way. A five pound rock held in the hand bespeaks coolness and passivity; yet it binds energy that, unleashed, could level a city.

Einstein banished space and time, banished momentum and energy, from any absolute and independent reality. The equivalence of mass and energy implied that mass, too, must be understood as a relative quantity. This means that a scientist on a train going by a ball park would measure a slightly different mass for a thrown ball than would another scientist sitting in the bleachers. The mass of an object depends on how fast it is moving. Einstein's famous equation, $E=mc^2$, is a shorthand representation of the dependence of an object's mass on its speed. Written out in full, the equation looks like this:

$$E = m(v)c^2 = \frac{m_0 c^2}{\sqrt{1 - v^2/c^2}}$$

This equation describes how the energy, *E,* of any object depends on its mass, *m*. The mass of the object in turn depends on its speed, *v*. The factor m_0 is known as the *rest mass* of the object. Rest mass is the mass of an object measured when it is at rest. This is the mass that a scientist would measure by placing an object on a scale in her laboratory. The concept of rest mass is a natural result of the fact that an object's mass depends on its speed.

The number *c*, the constant of relativity, provides a numerical factor with which to convert measures of length to measures of time, and measures of energy to measures of momentum. It also provides the conversion between measures of energy and measures of mass.

The equation $E=mc^2$ quantifies the huge amount of energy locked up in mass. The speed of light is already big and c^2 is a huge number: 90,000,000,000,000,000 in metric units. As any object's speed increases, its mass increases. As its speed approaches the speed of light, its mass becomes infinitely large. No massive object can ever be accelerated to the speed of light. It would take an infinite amount of energy to overcome the inertia of the ever-increasing mass.

Things do travel at the speed of light, however. Such entities are known as *massless* and light itself is their archetype. Although Maxwell thought of light as a wave, the quantum theory recognizes particles of zero mass as comprising a light wave. There are other massless particles as well. Because light travels at precisely *c*, and because *c* converts space and time units, light waves connect points in spacetime separated by a *zero interval.*

The elapsed time and separation in space between any two events in the universe can be described by a 4-vector. For example, the lifetime of an individual begins with birth at a specific moment in time and at a specific position in space and ends with death at another specific time and place. The distance between these two events in spacetime can be expressed with a 4-vector.

Interval is the technical name for the length of 4-vectors, representing the "distance" in spacetime between two events. Since the length of a 4-vector is the difference between its space and time components, there is the possibility of 4-vectors with zero length. This means that, for events separated by the zero interval, their separation in space is the same as their separation in time. The number *c* is used to convert between space and time measures. The path through spacetime connecting two such events is said to have a zero interval.

By virtue of its speed, every light wave connect points in spacetime that are separated by a zero interval. Therefore, when light bounces from an object to your retina, it traces a path of zero length in spacetime. Although the separation in space between object and eye can be enormous, the separation in spacetime can be zero. From the perspective of spacetime, everything you see is connected to you.

There is a wonderful underlying unity among things in our universe. The stars we gaze upon in the night sky are at enormous distances from us, yet we are connected to them in spacetime. All material objects are linked by light in this universe. The revolution of relativity forces us to rethink our ideas of separateness and motion, of our existence in space and time.

We see stars in the sky whose light has been traveling for thousands of years. Our cars throw beams from their headlights far out into the universe, beams that will travel forever through space. Because the light reflecting from our bodies can travel forever through space, we are fundamentally linked to all things past and future. Our perceptions of separation in space are illusory to a greater reality of connectedness.

As with many of the great revolutions in understanding, it was an act of spiritual courage to let go of ideas about absolute space and time, of ideas about unchanging mass. Space is not the fixed stage of existence. The curtain does not rise at the same time for everyone in the audience. Space and time are woven together in a web whose strands depend on motion. Yet by letting go of ancient notions and ideas, by trusting reason, we are shown a greater glory of unity and connectedness. We ascend a rung on the ladder that climbs toward the mind of the Creator.

Now we can understand why electrodynamics is a relativistic theory. Maxwell had discovered that the speed of light was related to the electric and magnetic constants. From simple experiments which measured the strength of electric and magnetic forces, Maxwell was able to deduce the speed of a light wave. Just as space and time or energy and momentum are complementary expressions of a single underlying reality, so are the electric and magnetic fields. The number c which provides the numerical translation between distance and time, between energy and momentum, also translates electric and magnetic forces.

Coulomb's law is the mathematical expression that describes the electric force generated by an electrically charged object. Ampere's law is the mathematical expression that describes the magnetic force generated by an electric current. An electric current is made up of charged particles in motion, electrons flowing in a wire, for example. With the realizations of relativity, the magnetic fields of electric currents are seen to be a relativistic effect of the electric fields of the individual electrons in motion.

As moving yardsticks become shorter, and moving clocks run slower, moving electric forces become magnetic forces. Magnetic forces are an expression of the geometry of spacetime manifesting in the motion of electrically charged objects. So it is not that c is derived from the electric and magnetic constants as originally calculated by Maxwell, but that the magnetic field and its constant, μ_0, are born from the relativistic distortion of Coulomb's law and its constant, ϵ_0.

Although it may seem that the speed of light is a number peculiar to electromagnetism because light is an electromagnetic wave, it is really that the propagation of electromagnetic waves is constrained by the relation of time and space in our universe; their speed must be c. The speed of light transcends electromagnetism. It is more like the dimensionless number π, which has been known for millenia. As π is a numerical property of space, c is a numerical property of spacetime.

If the electric and magnetic forces experienced by an electrically charged object depend on its state of motion, what is the underlying objective reality? The answer is that the motion of the object is the objective reality. The electric and magnetic forces conspire to enforce the objective reality, but there is no objective reality to the electric and magnetic forces individually.

Relativity provides a mathematical framework for insuring that physical law can be expressed in any state of motion. In the hypothetical naval exercise witnessed by Martians passing by at half the speed of light, both the Martians and the sailors on the ship can predict the trajectory of an artillery shell fired by the sailors. If that artillery shell were electrically charged, it would be deflected by the earth's magnetic field. The Martians and the sailors would measure different strengths of the magnetic field. But both would calculate the same trajectory. Electric and magnetic forces are both needed to calculate the trajectory of electrically charged objects, and their respective strengths depend on the state of motion of the scientist making the calculation, but they will always combine to predict the same trajectory for every scientist.

Coulomb's law describing the force between electrically charged objects is identical in mathematical form to Newton's law describing the gravitational force between objects with mass. Mass is the physical characteristic that implies participation in the gravitational field and electric charge is the characteristic that implies participation in the electric field. Indeed, mass is a source of gravitational force and electric charge is a source of electric force. Relativity allowed the magnetic force to be understood as a consequence of the electric force in motion. Is there a relativistic consequence of the gravitational force in motion? Is there a sort of gravitational magnetism?

The answer is yes. As with the theory of relativity described so far, this new theory of gravity was also provided by Einstein. It was known as *the general theory of relativity.* Although Einstein's early discoveries revolutionized understanding of mass and energy, of space and time, his greatest work still lay ahead: the general theory of relativity, finished in 1915. Its prediction of the bending of light by gravity was dramatically confirmed soon after and this success catapulted Einstein to an international superstar of science.

It cannot be said he was at all distracted by his stardom. After fleeing the Nazis in the 1930s, he spent the remainder of his years at Princeton, quietly working on his theories. He was an avowed pacifist and anti-militarist. He had a pure heart that could not conceive of the forces which drive societies to the madness of military escapades. He was always an ambassador for reason, peace, and non-violence. Einstein had the piety and demeanor of a devoutly religious man, and was the very icon of the new priesthood of mathematical dialog with the Creator.

While there was undoubtedly a deeply religious element to Einstein's character, its expression in terms of organized religion was for only a fleeting period of his life. For about a year, around age eleven, he experienced an intense period of obeisance to the precepts of Jewish faith. At this age, his school required him to study Catholicism, and he was taught Judaism at home by relatives.

His real epiphanies, however, were of science.[8] As an old man, he reflected back to when

> I experienced a miracle . . . as a child of four or five when my father showed me a compass . . . There had to be something behind objects that lay deeply hidden . . . the development of [our] world of

> thought is in a certain sense a flight away from the miraculous.[9]

Some years later, near the end of his childhood religious phase, epiphany struck again. He obtained a book on Euclidean geometry, which he referred to as the "holy geometry book." Einstein had found his religion, and never looked back to the more organized forms that absorb so many others. He saw himself as an instrument of holy revelation, believing that his gifts were not in navigating divine maliciousness, but in seeing the subtlety of the Lord.[10]

Thus Einstein was able to integrate his discoveries with the new meaning of religion. He authored this famous definition of the new religion, boiling Thomas Paine's message down into a few lines:

> A religious person is devout in the sense that he has no doubt of the significance of those superpersonal objects and goals which neither require nor are capable of rational foundation. . . a legitimate conflict between science and religion cannot exist . . . Science without religion is lame, religion without science is blind." [11]

For all the divine subtlety revealed in Einstein's earlier work, his general theory of relativity is an unparalleled expression of the sublime beauty of physical law. Mathematically, the general theory of relativity extended his previous work from the realm of constant velocities to accelerations. Einstein found that the force of gravity itself was inseparable from the coordinate systems of space and time in which we numerically describe motion. The gravitational field *is* the mathematical expression of the geometry, the shape, of spacetime.

Einstein showed how gravity arises as a result of the way physical law can be expressed in alternative coordinate systems. Martians and earthlings and any other alien beings, all moving in different coordinate systems, must be working from the same sheet of music, so to speak, of physical law. The mathematical form, as written on a piece of paper, must look the same for all states of motion. When one writes down an expression for any physical law which is the same for all coordinate systems and for all states of motion, one finds that there is a general mathematical construct in the equations which can be identified with gravity. The gravitational field is a force field which preserves the invariance of the mathematical form of physical law.

As it had for Einstein's earlier work on relativity, the geometrical interpretation of general relativity was to come later. Today, we speak of the force of gravity in terms of the curvature of space and time. The earth is moving straight and free through space, but the sun's mass has curved spacetime in such a way that the earth moves on a closed spatial loop – its orbit.

Although mathematically complex, Einstein's gravity derives from a simple principle: all objects move in straight lines through curved spacetime. These lines in curved space are called *geodesics*, from the term originated by mariners to describe the shortest path connecting any two points on the surface of the earth. The actual geodesic depends on the curvature of spacetime and its curvature manifests as the force we call gravity.

One can imagine the force of gravity metaphorically by thinking about mariners moving between ports of call along geodesics. If they for some reason did not realize that their ocean lived on a spherical earth, but they noticed that different constellations of stars came into view as they navigated around, they might deduce some strange force was pulling them around through space as they sailed over an ocean presumed to be flat. Yet when viewed from a higher dimensionality, there's no strange force; the mariner's path is merely affixed to a curved surface. Likewise, although spacetime looks "flat" wherever you are, it is curved over large distances. The earth doesn't know it is not moving in a straight path. It's just that the path is bent over large distances in space. The deviation of this path from being truly straight over such distances is what we call gravity.

Such a complex and subtle reformulation of gravity leads to predictions not present in the older view, such as the prediction of gravity bending light. Light does not have mass, so it would not even participate in Newtonian gravity. Yet gravity exerts an influence on light because gravity *is* the shape of spacetime through which light moves. Gravity bends spacetime and light moves through spacetime, so gravity bends light.

In his earlier work on relativity, Einstein was led to his astonishing discoveries by making some disarmingly simple and innocuous assumptions. As the basis for the general theory of relativity, Einstein assumed the equivalence of gravitation and inertia. This *equivalence principle* corresponds to the observation that no experiment can tell the difference between gravitation and accelerating motion. The acceleration of gravity at the earth's surface is about 10 m s^{-2} , meaning that the speed of a dropped object increases by 10 meters per second for each second of its fall. Someone doing experiments in a giant box far out in space, accelerating at 10 m s^{-2}, would record the same results as someone doing the same experiments on earth. The behavior of an object under the influence of an acceleration due to motion is called *inertia*. The acceleration due to gravity is indistinguishable from simple inertia.

Gravity and inertia play the same complementary roles as we saw for the electric and magnetic fields. There is an objective reality for objects moving in space and time. Two scientists working in two different coordinate systems might disagree about whether a gravitational field is present or whether an object is moving purely under inertia, but both must still calculate identical equations of motion for a given object.

The calculations of the behavior predicted in the objective reality may contain effects of gravity, or inertia, or any combination of the two. The objective reality of the object in motion must prevail.

Einstein's law of gravity is a mathematical construct that insures the laws of physics look the same in all coordinate systems, moving or otherwise. Newton's law of gravity, like his expressions for energy and momentum, is an approximation to Einstein's law for small masses and for speeds much smaller than light. The numerical predictions of general relativity have been exquisitely measured. There are no experimental results that cannot be explained within its framework.

The gravitational field of general relativity is much more complex than the electromagnetic field. A sense for the magnitude of this complexity can be gained by considering how many numbers are required to specify the gravitational field. The position of a buzzing fly, for example, requires 3 numbers to specify its position at each point in time: latitude, longitude, and altitude. In the same way, specification of both the electric and magnetic forces, at each point in space and time, requires 4 numbers. Newton's approximation to the fully relativistic gravitational field requires only a single number. Yet to completely specify the gravitational field of general relativity, at each point in space and time, requires 10 numbers.

Think of the complexity of the electromagnetic field underlying all human experience and all life on earth. Then realize there is even more complexity in the gravitational field. Many of the technological revolutions of the past century have emanated from an understanding of the electromagnetic field that began with Maxwell. Humanity has only begun to explore the gravitational field of Einstein.

Due to the differing strengths of the gravitational and electromagnetic forces, electromagnetic phenomena operate on a set of time scales, length scales, and mass scales vastly different than those on which gravitational effects manifest. Soccer players don't have to worry about the force of gravity between the ball and other players, for example. Since we are fundamentally electromagnetic beings, we are not conscious on the galactic length scales and 100-million-year time scales associated with the gravitational field. So we may never know the true flowering of the gravitational field in our universe any more than a barnacle can understand the life cycle of the whale on whose back it rides. It seems unlikely human consciousness based on electromagnetic phenomena, the firing of neurons in the brain, could ever know consciousness based on gravitational phenomena. They must inhabit such disparate realms of space, time, and mass.

The great lesson of relativity is that the pursuit of physical law has led to discoveries about the universe almost separate from physical law itself. We set out to understand the motion of the planets and end up learning undreamed truths of the nature of space and time, of mass and energy. Physical law is like the thread of Ariadne, left by the Creator for us to find, leading us step by step through the maze of our own physical reality.

But there was yet another jewel of truth hidden in the mathematics of general relativity. Einstein, who had unfailing confidence in the results of his previous revolutionary calculations years before they were verified experimentally, made a discovery in the equations of general relativity which he could not bring himself to believe. The result was so repulsive to him that he modified his otherwise beautiful field equations, adding an ad hoc term precisely tuned to cancel out the unwanted result. General relativity predicted the expansion of the universe.

Evolution

H is the number of universal evolution. The planets, the stars, and the galaxies are all evolving. Spacetime itself is evolving, manifesting in expansion of the universe. Peering through telescopes at the most distant galaxies deep in space, we see them receding from our own galaxy. *H* is the number which quantifies how fast the galaxies are receding. It was deduced after centuries of astronomical measurement, culminating in Hubble's discovery of the constant, *H*, which now bears his name.

An exquisite understanding of the light emitted by stars allowed astronomers to measure not only the shape and brightness of celestial objects, but also their distance, composition, and motion. The origin and destiny of all the things we see in the sky are known. The story of Creation has been told. The frontiers of human ignorance have been pushed back to the moment *before* Creation.

The night sky tapestry of light and pattern has fired the imagination of humankind for millenia. But it fell to Galileo to inaugurate human discovery outward from earth. Galileo revolutionized astronomy. Turning the newly-invented telescope toward the heavens, he discovered that the point of light we call Jupiter actually has a small entourage of moons. The four largest of these, which he discovered, are now known as the Galilean satellites. Although they are bright enough to be visible to the naked eye by themselves, they were lost to human perception all those millenia in the glare of Jupiter. So began the growth of human awareness outward from the home planet, with ever-more-powerful telescopes pushing human consciousness ever outward into time and space.

As Galileo discovered, many of the points of light visible to the naked eye are not points at all, but extended smears of light. Collectively, these smears of light were called *nebulae*. In the late 1700s, William Herschel built a powerful telescope and with it discovered the planet Uranus. It was the first discovery of a planet invisible to the unaided eye. Turning his telescope to the Milky Way, Herschel found it was composed of individual stars. Many of the nebulae discovered with earlier telescopes were also resolved by Herschel to be composed of individual stars. Although other nebulae, such as the Orion nebula, remained nebulous under Herschel's powerful eye, it was not unreasonable for him to assume that all nebulae were composed of stars. It was a just a matter of having a telescope powerful enough to resolve the constituent stars.

During the first centuries of telescopic astronomy, the craft was one of taxonomy: cataloging shapes, sizes, and positions. A rather large category of nebulae were found to be spiral in shape. They were discovered in all parts of the sky. These celestial pinwheels, the *spiral nebulae*, would be the objects through which *H* and the expansion of the universe were discovered.

The key to all astronomical discoveries lies in the fact that light is emitted and absorbed by substances at only a few precise frequencies, with a unique set of characteristic frequencies for each substance. The stars have a fingerprint of light and this fingerprint tells us their composition and motion. We know what the sun is made of without having to go take a sample from it. One of these characteristic frequencies, known as the ground state hyperfine frequency of hydrogen, is the most accurately measured quantity in nature: 1420405751.768 hertz. Pinpointing radiation of this frequency in the sky provides a celestial map of hydrogen. The same technique can be applied to different substances having different characteristic frequencies. The frequency fingerprint of a substance is called its *spectrum* and the individual frequencies are *lines*. So the hyperfine frequency is a single line in the spectrum of frequencies radiated by hydrogen. Just as strands compose a rope, so do spectral lines compose the light from stars and nebulae.

By measuring the light emitted by known substances in the laboratory, a catalog of spectra can be built, with line frequencies specified for each substance. This is compared with the spectra gathered telescopically from stars to determine the composition of each point of light in the sky. Although an understanding of why radiation was emitted and absorbed in lines would await the development of quantum theory in the 20th century, spectral studies of the stars and nebulae were already well underway by the mid-19th century.

An understanding of the frequency line spectrum provides information not only about the composition of a celestial object, but also about its motion. It is the discreteness of the radiation frequencies that makes this possible. If the point of light is in motion along the line of sight to earth, the apparent frequencies of its lines will be shifted a corresponding amount. An approaching point of light has its lines shifted toward higher frequencies, called a *blue shift.* A receding point of light has its lines shifted toward lower frequencies, called a *red shift.* These shifts in frequency are collectively known as *Doppler shifts*. For a moving object, each line in its spectrum will show the same Doppler shift in frequency compared to the spectral frequencies measured in the laboratory.

In 1868, an English amateur astronomer named William Huggins was able to determine the Doppler shift of the star Sirius, and therefore its motion along the line of sight to earth.

With this new measurement, astronomy moved from taxonomy to adventure.

In 1912, Vesto Slipher determined the Doppler shift of a few spiral nebulae. The spiral nebulae were all very faint objects. Splitting the light into spectral lines produced signals too faint for 19th century astronomers to measure. Slipher found that the spiral nebulae all exhibited rather large Doppler shifts, corresponding to velocities of several hundred or more kilometers per second.

While the Doppler shift of spectral lines provides a method for determining velocity, determining distance in the cosmos is a difficult undertaking and refinements continue to this day. A given star or nebula will appear to have some particular brightness when viewed from earth. But the same object would appear brighter if it were closer, dimmer if further. If all celestial objects had known absolute brightnesses, the distance could be easily inferred from its observed brightness. But not all celestial objects are the same. Additionally, their brightnesses can change with time. The Creator allows us precise information about the composition and velocity of the stars in the sky, but keeps their distances exceedingly difficult to determine.

The distance to a few nearby stars can be determined by how they appear to shift against background stars as the earth moves through space in its orbit around the sun. These are reliable direct measurements but are only valid out to a distance encompassing a very small minority of stars in the sky. To determine further distances requires some knowledge of absolute brightness. A crucial technique for such distance determinations was pioneered by Harlow Shapley.

The needed measure of absolute brightness came from a peculiar type of star known as a Cepheid, named after the prototype found in the constellation Cepheus. Astronomers were able to determine that Cepheids pulsate in brightness, and more importantly, the pulsation frequency is related to brightness. Astronomers can easily measure pulsation frequencies no matter how far a star may be. This pulsation allows calculation of an absolute brightness which, when combined with the brightness observed at earth, provides a measure of the distance. Shapley's contribution was to systematize this technique and obtain a precise relation between Cepheid pulsation period and brightness.

Shapley then used this powerful technique to determine the distances to large groups of stars called *globular clusters*. The globulars are quite ubiquitous in the sky, some visible to the unaided eye. They typically contain thousands of stars. With the powerful Mt. Wilson telescopes, Shapley was able to deduce a rough skeletal framework of the stars in the sky using the globular clusters as proxies. Although it was later found that he overestimated distances by about a factor of three, with these measurements the true size of the universe began to be appreciated.

But what of the spiral nebulae with their large velocities? Were they all inside Shapley's globular framework of stars? Or did some lie beyond the globulars? Many astronomers felt that perhaps the spiral nebulae were *island universes* of stars and that we were seeing them in the sky through our own island universe of stars which was previously mapped out by Shapley. Partially due to Shapley's overestimate of the distances to the globular clusters, there was no observational consensus about the island universe hypothesis. It seemed possible that perhaps the spiral nebulae were within the Milky Way after all. Such was the picture circa 1920.

Meanwhile, the interesting character of Edwin Hubble was undergoing life's transformations. He was a strong and energetic man of many interests. He balanced physics with track and baseball while at university. He balanced law studies with shot put and hammer throw while a Rhodes Scholar at Oxford. He apparently was so smitten with the mannerisms of upper-class English that he adopted them as his own, to the undying exasperation of his American colleagues. Returning from England to Kentucky, he passed the bar but never practiced law. Those legal skills would find use, however, in the court of scientific opinion.

After a stint teaching high school physics and basketball, and World War I service without overseas duty, Hubble hired on at Mt. Wilson, a mountaintop observatory outside a clear-skied Los Angeles. The Mt. Wilson 60-inch (1908) and 100-inch (1918) telescopes were engineering marvels, the world's best. Just as Hubble came to Mt. Wilson to undertake his great discoveries there, Shapley was leaving for a job at Harvard, not realizing until too late that he had left the fountainhead of astronomical discovery at a crucial time.

In the debate about the spiral nebulae, Shapley argued they were within our own island universe. Hubble took the next logical step of Shapley's work. He searched for Cepheids in the spiral nebulae with the 100-inch telescope. Hubble wrote Shapley in 1924 of the discovery of Cepheids in the Andromeda spiral nebula, proving that Andromeda was indeed an island universe outside the Milky Way. Shapley, upon receiving Hubble's communication, said, "Here is the letter that has destroyed my universe." The Shapley universe was not destroyed, just expanded enormously. The spiral nebulae were galaxies of stars in their own right, far outside our own galaxy.

Hubble had determined the scale of the universe. But this was only his first step in a series of observations and arguments leading toward the modern picture of an expanding universe. Hubble's great discovery was to be the systematic recession of the most distant galaxies. His partner in the discovery papers was Milton Humason, who initially started on at Mt. Wilson as a mule driver. Humason worked his way up to janitor, then relief night assistant. He so impressed the Mt. Wilson staff with his care and conscientiousness that he was promoted to a research position.

Hubble asked Humason to observe the fainter spiral galaxies in a systematic manner, to look for possibly larger recession velocities than those seen by Slipher. As Humason obtained velocities, Hubble obtained distances, and the first quantitative relation between the distance of a galaxy and its recession velocity was presented by them in 1929. Based on direct distance and velocity measurements for only 6 galaxies, plus an additional few dozen galaxies for which either distance or velocity only had been measured, Hubble delivered the fact of an expanding universe to an astonished world.

With Hubble's discovery, Einstein realized his mistake in doubting the most awesome prediction of his general theory of relativity: expanding spacetime. The man who had confidently predicted the conversion of mass to energy, the time dilation of moving clocks, and the bending of light by gravity, called his misplaced faith in a static universe his greatest blunder. Before

Hubble's discovery, he added an ad hoc term to his otherwise beautiful equations. The sole purpose of this additional term was to eliminate expanding spacetime as a solution to the equations of general relativity. In the end, expanding spacetime would prove to be the accepted explanation for the recession of the galaxies.

The decades since Hubble's discovery have seen only strengthening of the extraordinary concept of an expanding universe. Apparently, all the distant galaxies are receding from us at a speed which increases with their distance from us. That is what the Hubble constant *H* specifies: the rate of recession. The Hubble Space Telescope enabled *H* to be determined to unprecedented accuracy. That value is 72 km s^{-1} Mpc^{-1}.

A parsec (pc) is a unit of astronomical distance roughly equal to the distance traversed by light in 3 years of travel, or about 3 light years. A megaparsec (Mpc) is a million parsecs, a distance covered by a light wave traveling for over 3 million years. This value for *H* means that the recession velocity of the galaxies increases by 72 kilometers per second, about 160,000 miles per hour, for every million parsecs of their distance from earth. At the furthest distances, thousands of megaparsecs, galactic recession velocities approach the speed of light.

Although space and time are inflating, the material objects in our universe are not. The galaxies are like islands in an ever expanding ocean, but the islands themselves do not grow. The atoms and molecules in all material things are held together by electromagnetic forces. These forces maintain the size and shape of all matter in the arena of expanding space.

Vast distances in space are required to manifest the universal expansion, distances far beyond those of terrestrial experience. Looking out at the stars in our own galaxy, we do not see any pattern of recession. The stars in our galaxy are rather well-behaved, waltzing gracefully through space in orbit around the galactic center (where lurks a monster black hole with the mass of a million suns). The nearby galaxies, too, do not show any strong pattern of recession. Their motion is more or less random, with some of them moving toward us, some away. Our nearest large neighbor galaxy, Andromeda, for example, is falling toward the Milky Way. At these nearby distances, the galactic expansion velocity is no larger than the velocity of the sun in its orbit through our own galaxy and so is not noticeable.

But gazing out toward the more distant galaxies, a definite pattern sets in. All the galaxies are flying apart from each other. This pattern of recession is so dominant for the furthest galaxies that it is called the *cosmological flow*. We live in an exploding universe, an evolving universe.

After decades of scientific acceptance of the fact of galactic recession it is easy in our time to underestimate the revolutionary nature of its discovery. It took more than experimental evidence, to win acceptance of the fact of galactic recession. This is where Hubble's legal background came into play, making the case for acceptance of the velocity-distance relation to a skeptical community of astronomers. When further measurements over the ensuing decades only solidified the fact of recession of the galaxies, Hubble devoted the rest of his career to gathering the observational evidence necessary to choose from among the various theoretical explanations.

Hubble's own favored explanation for the recession of the galaxies was expanding spacetime as described by general relativity, the result that had been so repulsive to Einstein when he first discovered it in his equations. General relativity simply predicts that space and time may expand or contract, so that the distance between two objects in space can increase. In another explanation, Arthur Milne proposed that galaxies moving with random velocities in a non-expanding universe would tend to diffuse to larger distances from each other and from earth, with the fastest galaxies naturally being found at the largest distances from earth. Fritz Zwicky alternatively hypothesized that perhaps light is degraded by some unknown agency as it travels to earth, with the red shift owing to this loss of energy rather than to a Doppler shift arising from recession.

With these possibilities, it was by no means obvious that general relativity held the key to understanding galactic recession. Yet the other proven predictions of general relativity made its predictions about expanding spacetime impossible to ignore. The only problem was that the complexity of general relativity offers many expanding spacetime solutions, each with different properties. When the first attempts were made to theoretically explain galactic red shift, the correct mathematical solution for the spacetime of our universe was uncertain. In order to calculate a solution to the equations of general relativity, an assumption was needed.

The necessary assumption has no physical evidence to support it. It is purely a product of reason, even of good taste. It is a preference for choosing from among many possibilities that is informed by a scientist's sense of aesthetics. It is a mathematical assumption that flows from a qualitative sense of the nature of the divinity. At this point, physical law is constrained by a sociological preference. This assumption, this preference, this feeling for the beauty of physical law, is the *cosmological principle.*

The cosmological principle is a modern manifestation of the Copernican ethos. In essence, it is the assumption that no place in the universe is special. The universe is assumed to look the same in every direction, and have the same spacetime behavior everywhere. This is the simplest possible universe, and the most likely. The Milky Way lays no claim to any privileged location in our universe. The sun is a typical star among billions, in a typical galaxy among trillions.

The pre-Copernican would like to believe that earth is geometrically oriented in a special place, that the galaxies appear to be receding from earth because earth is at the center of the universe. But the spirit of reason has the courage to seek understanding of our universe within a framework of humility. Great advances come from seeing oneness and unity.

The cosmological principle greatly simplifies the mathematical task of obtaining solutions to the equations of general relativity which describe an expanding universe. This means that everything we see happening in the spacetime beyond earth is happening in every direction. This simple assumption allows us to complete the mathematical description of the expanding universe. It provides the basis of the "standard model" of the universe just as the assumption that the planets orbited the sun provided the basis for describing our solar system.

Hubble's discovery is only one manifestation of an expanding universe. Since the galaxies are now receding, they must have been closer together sometime past. In fact, extrapolating this motion implies Creation began as a singular explosive event known as the *Big Bang*.

When the universe was smaller, and the galaxies closer together, it was hotter. Since the Big Bang, the universe has cooled with its expansion. This cooling occurs because the expansion of the universe spreads the heat of the Big Bang over an increasingly larger volume of space. This heat is known as the *cosmic background radiation*. It has been measured with exquisite precision: the primordial fireball has cooled to 2.725 degrees Kelvin. In the coldest, emptiest, darkest part of space, the temperature is not at absolute zero. It is instead about 3 degrees above absolute zero. Just as the human body radiates heat at infrared frequencies, the body of the universe radiates cosmic heat at microwave frequencies. You can tune in the Big Bang at a frequency of 56.79 gigahertz on your radio.

The Hubble constant and the temperature of the cosmic background radiation are both quantitative reflections of the Creation. The Creation was not just the birth of matter *in* space and time, but the birth *of* matter, space, and time together. The galaxies are receding because they are embedded in spacetime, and the fabric of spacetime is expanding. The galaxies bob like corks in the currents of expanding spacetime.

The temperature of the cosmic background radiation has allowed the age of the universe, the time that has passed since the Big Bang, to be accurately measured at 13.7 ± 0.2 billion years. The moment of Creation was nearly 14 billion years ago.

The cosmic background radiation dates to an era when the universe had cooled enough and expanded enough that it became transparent to light. Before that time the universe was so hot and dense that light could not travel far. Now, starlight travels billions of light years. The time when the universe became transparent has been measured at 379 ± 8 hundred thousand years after the Big Bang. It took the universe nearly 400 thousand years to cool enough to become transparent to light.

Looking out into space is the same as looking back in time. We see the moon as it was just over a second ago, that sun as it was eight minutes ago. The cosmic background radiation is a view of the universe as it looked when it was only 3 tenths of 1 percent of its current age. Because the cosmic background radiation dates from the moment the universe became transparent, this moment is as far back as we can see with light. Yet we can pick out faint sources of light in the sky which reach back to the infancy of Creation.

Even without these cosmic discoveries we would at least know the age of the earth, which is about 5 billion years. Like the gift of line spectra which allows us to quantify the cosmos, there is peppered in the universe another gift for the intrepid explorer: the natural clocks of radioactive decay. All clumps of matter, including rocks, potsherds, petrified wood, and dinosaur bones, are embedded with microscopic clocks that tell us their age.

Many trace elements of everyday matter are radioactive, spontaneously decomposing into daughter elements. If you crack open a rock, for example, and find a small inclusion with both parent and daughter elements, their respective concentrations delineate the time elapsed since the parent was trapped in the rock. The time taken for this decay to occur varies from element to element. Some elements, like uranium, take billions of years to decay. These long-lived radioactive elements can show us the ages of rocks on the earth. Other elements have much shorter decay times, such as 10,000 years for carbon-14. These are the types of elements used to date ancient human civilizations and recently extinct creatures such as the woolly mammoth. Specific natural clocks can be used to date specific epochs. Through radioactive decay, our universe comes embedded with a whole palette of timepieces suitable to query any moment in the physical history of the earth.

In the 21st century, the scientific concept of evolution has become inseparable from the debate on the origin of human life. Yet Hubble's discovery shows that long before there was life in the universe, the matter composing it was evolving. In the aftermath of the Big Bang, there was only hydrogen and helium. The carbon, oxygen, and nitrogen necessary for life, and the silicon necessary for rocky planets, did not exist then. The elements necessary to constitute the earth were created by the evolution of the inanimate universe. It would be surprising to find life did not evolve, given that life performs on a stage which has itself been evolving since the beginning of time.

Under the influence of gravity, the primeval hydrogen born after the Big Bang was able to organize itself into large clumps of mass. Clouds of hydrogen formed stars and the stars formed galaxies. The first generation of stars in our universe were composed only of hydrogen. Left to themselves, stars create heavy elements from the fusion of lighter ones. Over the typical several-billion-year lifetime of a star, the immense pressures at its core will fuse hydrogen into helium, helium into carbon, and carbon into oxygen. This process will repeat onward and upward through the periodic table, all the way to iron. The release of energy from the fusion process is what makes stars shine.

If a star is massive enough, it consumes its nuclear fuel rapidly, burning brightly for a short period of time. It first builds up many onion-like layers of different elements, progressively heavier toward the center. After there is no fuel left to burn, the core cools and its pressure falls. The core is then unable to resist the gravitational burden of the outer layers and so it collapses. Like a dinner plate dropped on the floor releasing its gravitational energy into noise and flying fragments, a collapsing stellar core also releases energy, so much that it blows the entire star apart. Such an event is called a *supernova.* Some of these events yield an extremely dense object from the collapse called a *neutron star*. A neutron star is a ball of neutrons the size of a city, but weighing more than the sun.

In our galaxy of billions of stars there are only a few supernovae per century. Supernovae release enormous amounts of energy. A nearby supernova would be visible in broad daylight on earth. One too close would destroy the earth. During this catastrophic explosion, elements heavier than iron are synthesized all the way up to uranium. The blast blows newly-minted heavy elements out into space. Eventually, they condense, mix with other debris, and begin the cycle of star formation anew.

The second generation of stars, now rich with heavy elements from the stellar fusion of the hydrogen generation, is accompanied by rocky planets such as Earth, the Moon, Mars, Venus, and Mercury. Such planets could not exist while the universe was made only of hydrogen. The elements necessary for terrestrial life were manufactured in natural processes from the simple forms of matter initially born into our universe.

Matter evolved.

Stars and their planetary systems tend to organize into galaxies. Our own Milky Way galaxy is a spiral about 100,000 lightyears across but only a few thousand lightyears thick. It contains perhaps 100 billion stars. The Milky Way is a large galaxy with an entourage of dwarf galaxies in orbit around it. The galaxies in our neighborhood are part of a *Local Group* that is itself in orbit around the *Virgo supercluster* of galaxies. That whole system is falling into something called the G*reat Attractor.* But don't worry, you won't live to notice any changes. A human lifetime, even the whole history of humans on earth, is just a wink of an eye in galactic time. Our sun has not even made one trip in its orbit of the galaxy since mammals appeared on earth.

The earth and other planets in orbit around our sun were formed in a process of *bombardment.* Small bits of rock and ice condensed in the gigantic interstellar cloud of gas from which the sun was born. These bits then crashed together, forming bigger bits. As this process proceeded, progressively larger and more violent impacts created progressively larger objects. It is thought that at the end of the planet-forming era in our solar system, a Mars-sized object crashed into the young earth. The entire surface of earth became molten. The ejecta blown into space coalesced into the moon.

This process of bombardment and planetary formation has never really stopped. Every shooting star is a friendly vestige of this once fearsome process. Of course, every now and again a heavy hitter cruises through and gives the earth a mighty wallop, a reminder of how it used to be. The impact of an object 10 kilometers in size probably caused the extinction of the dinosaurs. Earth's fossil record is punctuated with such mass extinctions; many may have been catastrophic extraterrestrial impact events.

Forming a planet by bombardment releases a cosmic amount of heat. For a time the earth was covered with molten rock. The earth eventually cooled enough to form a skin of frozen rock on which we stand today. Gases were released from the hot interior, forming the earth's primitive atmosphere.

After over 10 billion years of dramatic evolution from pure hydrogen to a rocky planet with ocean and atmosphere, the matter in the universe had organized itself into a configuration suitable for terrestrial life.

The earth, the platform of life as we know it, is vibrant and dynamic. Its evolution continues to this day. The earth's crust is composed of several continent-sized plates of rock. The high ones make up the continents, the low ones hold the oceans. The ocean plates are transitory, as are the oceans they carry. A typical lifetime of an ocean is about 100 million years. This is the time for two continents to split apart, fill the void with ocean, and then close again in continental collisions. The collisions make mountains.

The process proceeds at speeds of about 1 cm per year. The Rockies, the Alps, and the Himalaya are getting taller. Lifelong residents of San Francisco die a meter closer to Tokyo. The Pacific Ocean is shrinking while the Atlantic is growing. Yet the alternating life cycles of oceans and mountains are still short enough, and the earth old enough, that some 50 generations of them have existed since the earth formed.

The energy that drives this remarkable evolution of the earth's surface is radioactive decay of elements inside the earth.

Our earth is heated, mountains are raised, and oceans are closed by the same processes of nuclear fission that drive nuclear reactors. The earth's interior could not have remained molten for this long without the power of radioactive decay.

Geologic processes are not the only processes affecting the evolution of the earth. Our planet has also been fundamentally altered by the life it sustains. The atmosphere earth had before life emerged on its surface is not the oxygen atmosphere we have today. The oxygen atmosphere necessary for animal life to evolve was created from the earth's proto-atmosphere by the first simple forms of life on earth. An oxygen atmosphere is the calling card of life. Left to itself and unsustained by organic processes, oxygen quickly reacts with other elements to produce inert compounds.

Life emerged quite early in the history of the earth, but for the first 3 or 4 billion years it consisted only of simple single-celled organisms. Around seven hundred million years ago, as measured by the radioactive clocks embedded in the rock, multicellular creatures appeared. No fossils appear in rock strata laid down before then.

That time in earth's history, just a few oceans ago, only a couple galactic rotations ago, was a magical moment. Multicellular animals emerged from this period in such a riot of forms that this point is marked as the *diversification of animals*. Life on earth diversified. In a relatively rapid series of changes, all the major unique forms of life appeared: vertebrates, land animals, conifer forests, insects, dinosaurs, mammals, flowering plants. The course of life on earth was to create the oxygen atmosphere and then roll an integrated organic carpet of plants and animals across earth's surface.

There is a beginning to Creation and we have found it. The Copernican revolution is often cited as a turning point in scientific history, launching our liberation from the notion of a geocentric universe. But the discovery of the exploding universe was of yet another order. While Copernicus encouraged us to contemplate a universe without humanity at its center, Hubble revealed something awesome about physical reality. He plumbed the enormous size of our universe. He saw into the depths of time. He saw that the universe always has been, and always will be, evolving. It was a discovery worthy of an adventurous, sea-faring species, ready to face what lies beyond the horizon.

Life has played a pivotal role in the physical evolution of the earth, but it is only one expression of that evolution. On the larger scale, evolution of the earth is just a part of the evolution of matter in our universe. Surely the surface of earth with its biosphere is one of the most complex physical environments in the universe. The complexity of the universe has progressed from raw hydrogen to whales and redwoods and humans. Where can evolution of the physical universe go next?

Perhaps consciousness is the next step in the evolution of our universe. The appearance of consciousness on earth was contingent on all other evolutionary processes, from the Big Bang to the creation of the earth to the diversification of animals. Consciousness is a step in the advancing evolution of the physical universe, the universe of matter and radiation. Consciousness seems to require matter, the matter of a human body. Yet consciousness also seems to transcend matter. Consciousness seems to be where evolution falls off the edge of matter.

To understand the connection between matter and consciousness, we turn to the last great revolution of physical understanding, the quantum theory. The grand project that started with Newton as a quantitative elucidation of the objective and immutable forces of nature ended up explicitly including consciousness in the formulation of physical law. Mind and matter are linked *mathematically* in the quantum theory.

Pilot Wave

By the time of Einstein's discovery of relativity, nature had revealed many secrets to ordinary mortals: that matter and radiation behaved as if obeying a small set of simple mathematical laws, that gravitational and electromagnetic force fields permeated the universe, exerting influence on the motion of material bodies, that space and time are woven together into the geometry of our universe, constraining the form of allowable physical law, and that the force we know as gravity is inseparable from that spacetime geometry.

This conception of physical reality, encompassing electrodynamics and relativity, is now referred to as *classical* physics. It is classical in recognition of the revolution in physical law that was to follow, a revolution ushered in by a small group of youthful physicists. Although these young revolutionaries didn't have long hair, their ideas certainly did. They created an interpretation of reality so alien to that which had existed before that it is no wonder such a leap had to be left to the youth of humanity, to those unafraid to see the world with fresh eyes. If electrodynamics and relativity were classical, then the quantum theory was rock 'n roll.

Quantitative investigations of the microscopic structure of matter began during the latter part of the 19th century. With these investigations came the gradual realization that physical law was as yet incomplete. There was a growing body of experimental observation not explainable in terms of classical physical law. For example, there was the fact that energetic atoms and molecules emitted electromagnetic radiation only at the discrete frequencies of spectral lines. There was a veritable zoology of different frequencies characterizing the known compounds, each compound having its own unique spectral fingerprint. Classical physics was not able to account for these spectra. The buzzword applied to the physics that would explain this discretization of frequencies was *quantum*.

The quantum revolution began with a whimper rather than a bang. It was more of a mathematical curiosity at first and started at the turn of the century with a German physicist named Max Planck who was investigating thermal radiation.

Any object with a temperature above absolute zero emits electromagnetic radiation over a range of frequencies and there is a peak frequency at which most of the radiation is emitted. As the temperature increases, so too does the peak frequency. The heating element of an electric stove, for example, gives off invisible infrared radiation as it warms up and then higher frequency visible light when it becomes “red hot”. The mathematical form of this spectrum of radiation, emitted by all objects at all temperatures, is independent of the shape or constituency of the emitting object. You only need to know its temperature to specify its spectrum of radiation. This thermal electromagnetic radiation pattern should have been accounted for by the theory of electrodynamics, yet attempts to describe it within that framework failed, and failed miserably. Electrodynamics could not account for the peak in the thermal spectrum, and instead predicted an infinite amount of energy would be emitted at the highest frequencies.

In 1899, groping for a mathematical solution to this problem, Planck found he could obtain an expression for the thermal radiation spectrum consistent with observation if he assumed that the radiation was emitted in discrete bits – *quanta* of radiation. That is, the energy given off as electromagnetic radiation was not infinitely divisible. There was, instead, some fundamental unit of electromagnetic energy. The total energy given off by the radiating object was a large *integer* multiple of this basic unit of electromagnetic energy.

To calibrate his radiation formula with observations, Planck introduced a constant. This constant now bears his name and is commonly written as $\hbar$. Planck's constant would turn out to be fundamental to the nature of our universe. Unlike the electric constant $(4\pi\epsilon_0)^{-1}$ and the gravitational constant G, the Planck constant $\hbar$ is not associated with any force of nature. Rather, it is more like the speed of light c, expressing something of the *fabric* of our universe.

In 1905, the same year he discovered relativity, Einstein extended Planck's results to establish the quantum description of light. The problem treated by Einstein was the photoelectric effect, in which light striking a surface generates electric current. Einstein identified the quantum of light, now known as the *photon*, and determined that a photon's energy is given by the product of $\hbar$ and its frequency. This particle description of light was complementary to its classical description as an electromagnetic wave and was the first indication of the *wave-particle duality* in nature. The matter and radiation that inhabit our universe have aspects to them that are both wave-like and particle-like. We need both frameworks to describe nature.

Because $\hbar$ does not appear in electrodynamics, it was clear that a new physics was dawning. Somehow classical electrodynamics failed to account for the quantum nature of light. Electrodynamics must be an approximation to some deeper theory of radiation. Into this fertile time of scientific exploration stepped a figure who would become both father and midwife to the birth of the quantum theory.

In 1913, at the age of 28, Niels Bohr made a name for himself by constructing the first quantum model of the hydrogen atom which successfully accounted for its unique spectrum of electromagnetic radiation. At the turn of the century it wasn't clear what atoms were made of, although electrons and nuclei were known at the time. It was, however, known that these particles were electrically charged. But if your conception of the atom involved electrons in orbit around a nucleus, like planets in orbit around the sun, classical electromagnetic theory predicted the electrons would rapidly radiate away all their energy and spiral into the nucleus. Then atoms would collapse and matter (which is mostly empty space) could not exist at all. Although we still think of atoms as electrons in orbit around a nucleus composed of protons and neutrons, it is now recognized that it is the wave nature of electrons which allows matter to exist stably. But during those early years, the wave nature of matter was still undiscovered.

Bohr proposed a model of hydrogen in which the atom is composed of an electron in orbit around a proton. He also assumed the orbits are stable, that they will not radiate away, an assumption in violation of the known laws of electrodynamics. Bohr was the first to propose suspending the classical laws of electrodynamics for atomic phenomena.

While this assumption seems inescapable in retrospect, it was a bold stroke in 1913.

With his model of the hydrogen atom, Bohr initiated the overthrow of classical electrodynamics as a fundamental theory of nature. Such an overturning of accepted physical law rarely happens in science and represents nothing less than a crisis of understanding. Until 1913 the history of physical law was characterized by a growing depth of understanding, a series of increasingly accurate models of reality, but never a complete repudiation of previously accepted theory. Every previous theory of physical law had been found to be true for every system of matter and energy explored by humankind. The fact that Bohr's theory was accepted by the community of physicists is testament to the desperate state of physical law in 1913. The Bohr model was so successful at explaining the spectrum of the hydrogen atom that it was apparent there was a kernel of truth to it. It propelled physicists on the road to the quantum theory and a complete revision of an understanding of reality over 200 years old.

The Bohr model was, however, only successful for

hydrogen, the simplest atom. The model did not work for helium, implying that Bohr's model was incomplete if not incorrect.

The first incarnation of quantum theory, known as non-relativistic quantum mechanics, was not formulated until 1925. It was discovered independently and almost simultaneously by Erwin Schrödinger and by Werner Heisenberg. Heisenberg worked closely with Max Born, Pascal Jordan, and Wolfgang Pauli, who accomplished many of the basic calculations in Heisenberg's theory. In 1928 Paul Dirac formulated the first quantum theory consistent with special relativity, thereby predicting the existence of anti-matter. The flash of discovery surrounding quantum theory makes one wonder whether great times bring forth great men or if human capability is always present, just lying dormant until the moment of need. Humanity was ready for divine understanding and it was crystallized in a small group of people.

Bohr's work in 1913 was the first major step along the road to a quantum theory of matter. His role in the ensuing two decades would be not one of accomplishment, but rather one of facilitation. By 1925, the birth year of modern quantum theory, Bohr had a Nobel prize under his belt and had founded one of Europe's leading institutes for the study of quantum physics in Copenhagen. He was a figure of worldwide prestige on a par with Einstein.

Heisenberg, Pauli, Dirac, and Jordan, on the other hand, were in their early twenties. They, too, would all earn their share of fame and prestige in physics. At the time they were creating quantum mechanics, however, Bohr was the master and Copenhagen the Mecca for the young pilgrims of the new quantum theory of matter.

Among physicists, some are more mathematically inclined than others. Bohr was a philosopher. After his early work, it became common for him to publish scientific papers containing not a single mathematical equation. To indulge this predilection while maintaining credibility in the field of theoretical physics was a feat that will probably not be repeated. Perhaps because of their lack of explicit mathematics, Bohr's papers were notorious for being difficult to understand. Yet his stature was unparalleled.

The physicist James Franck, who came to Copenhagen, was quoted as saying,

> Bohr's wisdom and his complete freedom from conceit . . . created such deep respect and admiration in the young physicists that it bordered on hero worship.[12]

Schrödinger, only two years younger than Bohr, saw this phenomenon a little differently:

> There will hardly again be a man who will achieve such enormous internal and external success, who in his sphere of work is honored almost like a demigod by the whole world, and who yet remains – I would not say modest and free of conceit – but rather shy and diffident like a theology student. I do not necessarily mean that as praise, it is not my ideal of a man. Nevertheless this attitude works strongly sympathetically compared with what one often meets in stars of medium size in our profession . . .[13]

Percy Bridgman, another physicist of that era, said,

> I have seldom met a man with such evident singleness of purpose and so apparently free from guile . . . I know from many sources that Bohr makes the same impression on others . . . and he is now idolized as a scientific god through most of Europe.[14]

Einstein characterized Bohr as,

> like one perpetually groping and never like one who believes he is in possession of definite truth.[15]

In addition to humility and kindness, bravery and principle

were elements of Bohr's charisma. When the Nazis came crashing into Denmark, Bohr refused numerous offers for refuge. He chose instead to remain behind with the Danes, supposing he could do more good for them in Denmark than in Britain or America. Yet during the years leading up to the occupation of Denmark, he worked tirelessly to secure the escape from Nazi terror of Jewish and refugee scientists throughout Europe.

His decision to remain was especially heroic given the misconception among military and political officials of Britain, Russia, and Germany that Bohr somehow held the key to the ongoing development of nuclear weapons. By the late 1930's, Bohr was philosopher-king of the community of physicists and undoubtedly privy to the investigations of a global network of scientists. But he was not an essential player in the effort to construct the atomic bomb, and aside from some pre-war work on the structure of the nucleus, was not on the forefront of those developments. The Italian Enrico Fermi, on the other hand, was able to use his recent Nobel prize to escape the fascists, apparently without raising an eyebrow. Fermi then went on to personally build the world's first nuclear reactor as part of the Manhattan project.

When Bohr did finally make it to Britain and America, however, he lent his prestige to the Manhattan project. His escape was prompted when a high Nazi official warned the Jews of Denmark that they were to be deported to the death camps. Bohr and nearly the entire population of 8,000 Danish Jews managed to escape across the sea to Sweden in boats of every description while a sympathetic German naval officer kept his fleet in port. From there, British Intelligence smuggled Bohr to Britain in an airplane made of plywood. The absent-minded professor somehow neglected to don his oxygen mask for the ascent to 20,000 feet, passed out from oxygen deprivation, and slept through the entire flight.

The story of the role of atomic scientists during World War II is a fascinating and complex one that is told elsewhere. One poignant episode in that drama that is worth mentioning was the isolation of Heisenberg. He was the most famous scientist to remain in Nazi Germany. Indeed, he headed up research on nuclear energy during that time. The record shows that

Heisenberg was able to quash the development of a Nazi atomic bomb by arguing against its feasibility, while he himself knew the opposite to be true. He instead argued for a limited research program into the development of atomic energy and worked to build a reactor. His goal was to preserve as much as possible of physics in Germany and to keep young German physicists out of combat, with an eye toward rebuilding German science after the war.

But Heisenberg's colleagues, and Bohr in particular, never forgave his allegiance to Germany and wrongly believed that Heisenberg had tried to build an atomic bomb for Hitler. During the Nazi occupation of Denmark, Heisenberg visited Bohr to suggest the world's physicists try to hide the monstrous possibility of atomic weapons from their military patrons. Heisenberg thought that at that crucial moment in history the physicists were in a position to strangle atomic terror in the cradle. Bohr was shocked by this suggestion, thinking Heisenberg a Nazi trying to keep the Allies from working on the bomb after Hitler had driven from Europe those most capable of the task. The irony is that the Allied scientists considered Heisenberg morally bankrupt for remaining with Germany while at the same time harboring self-doubts about the horror they had consented to bring into the world with the Manhattan project.

Those questions of morality were never resolved by the participants, even decades after the war. But twenty years before the war those same men, led by Niels Bohr, were up to the task of deciphering the fundamental nature of reality. It was not Bohr's kindness, not his humbleness, and not his scientific genius that so influenced the understanding of reality that persists to this day. Instead, it was his relentless and ruthless demand for clarity in the search for truth. Through the use of both his prestige and his tenacious force of character, Bohr exerted considerable influence on the subsequent direction and development of the quantum theory. The developers of quantum mechanics were confined to and traveled between a very few European institutes, and Copenhagen was one of them.

Dirac recalled,

> . . . we had long talks together, very long talks, in which Bohr did practically all the talking.[16]

After a decade of searching for an understanding of the atom which would surpass Bohr's model, the breakthrough came in 1925 at the hands of 23-year-old Werner Heisenberg. Here, as with relativity, physical law forced a re-appraisal of our conceptions of physical reality. Similar in spirit to Bohr's bold strokes a dozen years earlier, Heisenberg's great insight was to do away with the *concept* of atomic orbits. Instead, argued Heisenberg, physics must be based on *observables*, and atomic orbits are not **observable**. We can never follow the electron around in its orbit in the same way that we can follow the moon around its orbit. Instead, scientists infrequently peer into the atom and deduce something about an electron.

We can never see the things that make up atoms. They are smaller than the wavelength of light and we can never "take a picture" of them. We can only deduce things about subatomic particles. We can only instantaneously measure the positions of subatomic particles at discrete instances, like checking the ID of a passenger at a subway stop. Since these particles are not continuously visible to our eyes or our measuring instruments, we cannot assume that between measurements the particle was following a continuous trajectory connecting its observed positions.

The concept of motion as a smooth continuous trajectory through space may be valid for planets, baseballs, and other “large” objects with which humans are familiar, but it does not describe the behavior of atomic phenomena. Nature will not allow the luxury of assuming that just because a particle may be sighted at point A and point B, it has traversed the intervening distance. It's a reasonable assumption but nature won't abide it.

So, instead of the simple continuous trajectory expected from classical physics, Heisenberg described the position of an electron in a hydrogen atom with a set of possible numerical values in terms of a mathematical entity known as a *matrix*. The position of an electron cannot be chosen from any point on the number line. There are only a few special values that the position can take. This description of matter, pioneered by Heisenberg, Max Born and Pascal Jordan, became known as *matrix mechanics*. The concept of position changing continuously in classical mechanics is replaced by a matrix of discrete position values.

One famous result of the matrix mechanics, and of all quantum theories, is that our knowledge of any atomic system contains unavoidable uncertainty. We can never have the perfect knowledge of such a system that we can have for, say, the moons of Jupiter. By performing experiments to gain information about an electron's position, we disturb its momentum. To determine this modified momentum, its position is then disturbed. We can never with certainty know both the position and momentum of atomic particles. There is apparently an underlying uncertainty about the physical state of all matter that our understanding of physical law can not yet transcend.

A few months later in 1925, Wolfgang Pauli used the matrix mechanics to derive the hydrogen spectrum, sealing the displacement of the Bohr model by the new quantum theory. The end of the Bohr theory was the beginning of a rich harvest of physical understanding in the fertile fields of quantum theory. Unknown to the scientists riding the quantum wave in 1925, they were hurtling toward a profound understanding of the wave nature of matter.

Two years earlier, in 1923, the 31-year-old Frenchman Louis de Broglie had suggested a wave behavior for electrons that closed the circle of symmetry with Einstein's 1905 hypothesis of a particle nature for light. Einstein showed how light, which we had become used to thinking of in terms of waves, exhibits some of the characteristics of particles. De Broglie provided simple mathematics to show that matter, which we had become used to thinking of in terms of particles, exhibits some of the characteristics of waves. In fact, De Broglie earned the Nobel prize for his doctoral thesis on this subject.

De Broglie simply proposed that anything we might call a particle, matter or light, electron or photon, has a wavelength and a frequency. The energy e of this particle is related to its frequency ν by the relation Einstein discovered for photons: $e=\hbar\nu$. Also, the momentum p of every particle is related to its wavelength λ: $p=\hbar\lambda$. Light waves can behave like particles. Particles can behave like waves. This is the wave-particle duality of nature.

$1.054571597\text{x}10^{-34}$ kg m^2 s^{-1}

In 1923, it was still unclear exactly what was "waving" with de Broglie's matter waves. For light waves, it is the electromagnetic field. But what is an "electron wave" when an electron is such a small particle, confined in the small space of an atom?

In 1925, 38-year-old Erwin Schrödinger introduced an alternative mechanics from which he was able to calculate the hydrogen spectrum. Schrödinger built on de Broglie's work by describing an electron in a hydrogen atom using the mathematics of waves, a picture developed independently of Bohr and Heisenberg. The electron wave was called the *wave function.* Schrödinger's quantum theory became known as *wave mechanics,* in contrast to Heisenberg's matrix mechanics.

The discrete numbers of the hydrogen spectrum could be described in terms of standing waves in the atom, just like the standing waves on a guitar string. The need for a matrix of position values had apparently abated. Where Heisenberg's matrix mechanics seemed to describe a grainy, discontinuous reality, Schrödinger's wave mechanics seemed to describe a continuum.

However, the wave and matrix mechanics were soon discovered to be mathematically equivalent and complementary expressions of quantum theory. They had successfully replaced classical mechanics for understanding the atom. But during those early days, the wave mechanics met with greater favor among physicists, partly because the mathematics of matrices was relatively unfamiliar to them. Heisenberg himself was unaware of the body of mathematical work on matrices. After he learned about it from Born and Jordan, he took a few months getting up to speed.

Another reason for preferring the wave mechanics was that the discontinuities apparently implied by the matrix mechanics were counter-intuitive, not only to the existent body of classical physics, but also to common sense. Physicists in 1925 were wedded to their conceptual pictures of smooth trajectories in space and time; the wave mechanics at first seemed to accommodate this predilection.

Schrödinger's view was that waves are the basic reality and particles only derivative to them. The particles were “conceived as wavepackets”. He thought these matter waves would be a mere extension of classical physics. Like the electromagnetic field, there existed a matter field. An electric or magnetic force is viewed as a wave on the sea of the electromagnetic force field. The electron was to be viewed as some sort of fluctuation on the sea of the matter field.

This hope was shattered in 1926 when Max Born identified the wave function as a *probability* wave, not a matter wave. He realized that Schrödinger got the mathematics right but had misinterpreted the meaning of the matter waves. Born answered the question of what is doing the waving in the wave function of the electron – it is *probability*. The wave function was not the field of a physically measurable quantity like the electromagnetic field, but the probability of obtaining a given value in a given measurement.

Everything we can know about an electron is obtained through measurements. We can measure an electron to determine its position in space or energy at an instant of time. Repeated measurements on identical systems would yield a range of possible results and the wave function describes the probability of obtaining a particular result.

The wave function is a strange bird in physics. From 1926 to the current day, it has raised all sorts of philosophical questions about its physical meaning, its relation to the world of human experience, and about what is knowable in physics. The wave function opens a door into a wholly new and heretofore unseen level of reality. Classical physics was the story of fields that pull a skydiver to earth or keep a satellite in orbit. It was the story of fields that could turn a compass needle or spawn a lightning strike. No one had to argue about the meaning of these fields. With the quantum mechanics, the group of young scientists had not only discovered a new field in the wave function but also had to figure out what this field really meant. Fields of force are the familiar inhabitants of physical law. Where is there room for a field of probability? The theory is very successful but what does the wave function mean?

Bohr, with his philosophical bent, took great interest in the *interpretation* of the wave and matrix mechanics, of quantum mechanics. It was Heisenberg, Pauli, Born, Jordan, Dirac, and Schrödinger, who developed the explicit mathematical theories we know as quantum mechanics. Bohr played the role of wise mentor, question asker, and facilitator. But he orchestrated the consensus on the interpretation of the quantum theory with an iron fist of persistence in a velvet glove of humility. Heisenberg recalled one incident of heated debate with Bohr about his own ideas regarding the interpretation of quantum mechanics, which he was preparing for publication:

> Bohr tried to explain that it was not right and I shouldn't publish the paper. I remember that it ended by my breaking out in tears because I just couldn't stand this pressure from Bohr.[17]

Perhaps Heisenberg's youth made him particularly susceptible to the power of Bohr's influence, but even the elder Schrödinger suffered. Heisenberg also recalled:

> The discussions between Bohr and Schrödinger began already at the railway station in Copenhagen and were continued each day from early morning until late at night. Schrödinger stayed in Bohr's house and so for this reason alone there could hardly be an interruption in the conversations. And although Bohr was otherwise most considerate and amiable in his dealings with people, he now appeared to me almost as an unrelenting fanatic, who was not prepared to make a single concession to his discussion partner or to tolerate the slightest obscurity. It will hardly be possible to convey the intensity of passion with which the discussions were conducted on both sides, or the deep-rooted

> convictions which one could perceive equally with Bohr and with Schrödinger in every spoken sentence. . . So the discussion continued for many hours throughout day and night without a consensus being reached. After a couple of days, Schrödinger fell ill, perhaps as a result of the enormous strain. He had to stay in bed with a feverish cold. Mrs. Bohr nursed him and brought tea and cakes, but Niels Bohr sat on the bedside, and spoke earnestly to Schrödinger: "But surely you must realize that . . ."[18]

Even in topics unrelated to quantum interpretation, Bohr's influence was irresistible. His colleague, James Franck, recalled:

> . . . Bohr did not allow me to think through whatever I did to the end. I made some experiments. And when I told Bohr about it, then he said immediately what might be wrong, what might be right. And it was so quick that after a time I felt that I am unable to think at all . . . Bohr's genius was so superior. And one cannot help that one would get so strong inferiority complexes in the presence of such a genius that one becomes sterile.[19]

The result of constant contact with Bohr and the concomitant exposure to his forceful personality was to be assimilated into his way of thinking. Abraham Pais remarked in his definitive biography of Bohr that it was not always easy for younger people to cope with the immense power of Bohr's personality.[20]

For the first time in the history of physical law a quantitative understanding of nature was gained for which there was no obvious corresponding qualitative understanding of the meaning of the new theory. As happens so often in the course of physical law, the great discoveries were made by young people. They were mathematically sophisticated enough to discover the new physical law but not emotionally sophisticated enough to resist pressure from their mentor, pressure to yield to his interpretation of the meaning of what they had found. At this remarkable instant in the history of physical law, Niels Bohr stood poised to pioneer not mathematics, but meaning.

At the 1927 Solvay Congress of the world's top physicists, de Broglie presented a *pilot wave* interpretation of the wave function. De Broglie suggested that the wave function was a real physical field that affected the motion of material objects. He proposed that it was a discovery of a kind with the electric and gravitational fields. Indeed, the Schrödinger equation can be mathematically recast to reflect this view. De Broglie's interpretation withered under the direct objections raised by

Pauli, which he was unable to convincingly repudiate. It expired under the indifference of Schrödinger and Einstein, the only two physicists with the prestige to take on Bohr and his disciples. One of the Solvay Congress attendees, Paul Ehrenfest, recalled from that meeting:

> BOHR towering completely over everybody. At first not understood at all . . . then step by step defeating everybody.[21]

The situation led physicist Arnold Sommerfeld to describe Bohr as the "director of atomic theory."[22]

Bohr was a force that altered the scope and direction of physical law. The human conception of physical law had moved, with the advent of quantum theory, out of a realm of cold objectivity into one of interpretive subjectivity. And Niels Bohr, the right man in the right place at the right time, had a profound influence on the integration of the quantum theory into the human interpretation of physical reality, and by implication, on the future directions of scientific investigation.

The time of Bohr's dominance of physical law was the first time in the history of physical law that the ultimate nature of reality was up for debate. It was a unique time in the history of physical law because the discovery of quantum mechanics required a separate law-giver to explain the meaning of it all. The hope for an objective reality, for a story independent of the story teller, had appeared finally to end. Niels Bohr would decide the ultimate nature of reality.

It is no wonder that the standard interpretation of quantum mechanics is known as the *Copenhagen interpretation*. Only Einstein could match Bohr in stature at the time, even though in hindsight one would expect Heisenberg, Pauli, Dirac, Schrödinger, Born, de Broglie, and others to have been as qualified for "quantum interpretation" as Bohr. The Copenhagen interpretation would become so entrenched in the policy and practice of physics that one author called it the Copenhagen hegemony.

We turn, then, to a description of quantum mechanics and its Copenhagen interpretation. What is remarkable about Copenhagen is that for the first time in the formulation of physical law, human consciousness enters the mathematical form of the equations at a fundamental level. It is, truly, a link between mind and matter, although not a *useful* link, according to Copenhagen.

The speed of light, *c,* is a fundamental constant in the theory of relativity. Quantum theory also has a fundamental constant: Planck's constant, $\hbar$. The speed of light relates distance to time in the spacetime geometry of our universe. Planck's constant characterizes the granularity of matter and energy in our universe. It is the same granularity seen in the discrete energies of a line spectrum.

The essence of quantum theory is that material particles actually behave as waves. These waves are a measure of the probability of a particle being in a given *state*. The state of a microscopic particle includes its position, momentum, and other quantities of interest. The wavelength and frequency of these probability waves are as first described by de Broglie. The wave function is the probability wave that describes the quantitative destiny of any particle. Every particle has its own wave function, and every system of particles has a composite wave function. There is even a wave function for the universe! Most importantly, according to the Copenhagen interpretation, everything we can know about a particle is embedded in its wave function. The wave function is a mathematical book of destiny for any material thing, circumscribing the envelope of its potentiality.

Mathematically, the wave function describes all possible states of existence. The wave function also allows for uncertainty among various possible states. Imagine, for example, talking to your brother on the phone while he was in New York. If he said he would be going to Boston sometime later, his wave function would include a part describing him in Boston, with some probability, and a part describing him in New York, with some probability. In the same way, the wave function is a mathematical dictionary of possibility.

As an atomic illustration of the wave function, consider the example of radioactive decay. The wave function of a uranium atom may contain a possible destiny of decay to a thorium atom and another destiny of continued stability as uranium. The relative probability between these two possibilities would explain the amount of thorium decay from a large sample of such atoms.

There are two ways that a wave function can evolve in Copenhagen quantum mechanics. Curiously enough, the difference depends on whether or not the system described by the wave function is being **observed.** The use of bold font emphasizes that Copenhagen insists upon a special philosophical meaning for this word. An **observation** has occurred when somebody, or some mind, measures something.

Our measurements of atomic phenomena are like snapshots of an ever churning ocean. Measurements occur relatively infrequently and atomic systems spend most of their time **unobserved**. For these times there is an equation of the type one has come to expect from physical law. This equation tells us how the wave function, written $|\psi\rangle$, will change with time. This equation was originally discovered by Schrödinger, it involves $\hbar$, and its predictions have been verified experimentally to as many digits as you care to measure. The form of Schrödinger's equation is compact, relating the change in time of the wave function to its energy content. Here's what it looks like:

$1.054571597 \times 10^{-34}$ kg m^2 s^{-1}

$$i\hbar \frac{d}{dt} |\psi\rangle = H|\psi\rangle$$

The deceptively simple form of Schrödinger's equation belies a wealth of mathematical complexity. It also exhibits that hallmark of the quantum theory, explicit reference to the complex number i in the equations of physical law. We don't need to know where this equation comes from in order to design a transistor with it. It's enough to know it works. As a mathematical recipe for calculation, the Schrödinger equation will be around until phenomena are discovered which do not conform to its predictions.

When a particle is not being **observed**, its wave function is evolving in a well-understood way. The wave function is described by the Schrödinger equation as well as electromagnetic waves are described by the Maxwell equations. But when a particle is **observed**, a catastrophic condition arises for its wave function. The act of **observation** is said to *collapse* the wave function. The wave function of a particle seems to depend on whether or not it is **observed**.

In practical terms, this means that whenever a scientist

makes a measurement of some aspect of an atom, that knowledge collapses the wave function of possibilities for that atom. All possible destinies for the atom are zeroed out in the wave function, save for that which was realized in the measurement.

It is taken as an article of faith in the Copenhagen interpretation that the state into which an atom collapses upon **observation** is unpredictable. The wave function can only tell what the *probability* is of the atom ending up in some particular state.

If you are willing to accept that **observation** is an act of mind, then here is the link between mind and matter in physical law. It is an undeniable aspect of the Copenhagen interpretation that observation affects the wave function by collapsing it. The wave function is the mathematical quantity that describes the worlds of physical possibility for a given system of matter. Since the act of **observation** is a choice of mind, mind and matter are linked through the wave function.

The Schrödinger equation hews to the form we have come to expect for physical law: force fields described by differential equations. But to include a caveat that this new field, the wave function, collapses when **observed** requires augmenting the theory in a non-mathematical way. The theory has to single out those special times when the human choice to **observe** is made, and proclaim that the Schrödinger equation only holds otherwise. In other words, the Schrödinger equation has a caveat.

In one standard textbook on quantum mechanics, this suspension of Schrödinger's equation during **observation** is given a dignified name: "the 5th postulate". After the mathematical elegance of electrodynamics and general relativity, it is disconcerting to see physical law with applicability conditions. Such non-mathematical statements of physical law hearken back to ancient Greek or Roman conceptions of natural law or perhaps to those of medieval alchemists. No previous mathematical physical law was encumbered with postulates about when an equation of physical law applies. Electrodynamics and general relativity are purely mathematical. You can literally write their governing equations in a few lines. All conclusions and implications are purely mathematical derivations. This is not so with Copenhagen quantum theory.

One might think mind affecting matter in physical law would be heralded as the promise of undreamed mastery over the material world. But according to the Copenhagen interpretation, there is a hitch. Copenhagen contends that the influence of **observation** on the wave function is fundamentally uncontrollable. So, while Copenhagen admits that mind does affect matter, it is taken as gospel that the effect is uncontrollable. Mind affecting matter is merely a philosophical curiosity, of no possible practical import.

These aspects of the meaning of quantum theory have been debated since 1925. It is astounding that, whatever the merits of this debate, physical law has progressed to the point where such debate becomes unavoidable. Mathematical physical law has almost transcended its cold, numerical precision to portend something of a spiritual revelation, a connecting dialog between the One and the All.

Framed against such lofty possibilities, the Copenhagen interpretation of reality is rather minimalist. It is based, first and foremost, on recognition of a reality beyond human comprehension or expression. Human language and human concepts are inherently limited, argued Bohr, and we may ask questions of nature which yield strange, non-intuitive answers. The answers may seem strange because we humans are constrained by our thinking in terms of classical concepts. Scientists tend to build physical law in the same terms in which they think. But nature is not constrained by human common sense.

The thing called the wave function is useful because it contains the answer to any question an experimenter can ask. It provides the probability of a given measurement yielding a given value, even though consecutive experiments may require viewing an electron as first a particle, then a wave. For Niels Bohr, the fundamental reality was the electron-plus-observer, for no observation could be predicted from quantum mechanics without first specifying the experimental setup. So there must be no speaking about the electron, about its inherent reality, until a human mind is joined to it through an experiment. There is no reality for the electron without its **observation.** There is no reality for anything until it is **observed**.

When these concepts are extrapolated to macroscopic phenomena, they appear to deny the very existence of any objective reality. Instead, everything floats in a sea of unrealized potential. If the new quantum philosophy is applied to the moons of Jupiter discovered with space probes, those moons would not have existed until we finally **observed** them. The Galilean moons of Jupiter would not have existed until Galileo found them through his telescope. Yet they are as old as anything in our solar system. The lack of existence prior to human **observation** should not conjure up images of the void. Rather, they existed in some strange quantum world of possibilities. The act of human **observation** brought forth a single one of those possibilities into objective reality. Human consciousness collapsed the wave function of the moons of Jupiter.

Besides the apparent abandonment of objective reality at the quantum level, the quantum theory demands another radical departure from the usual assumptions underlying physical law. The shocking idea is that the wave function is merely a reservoir of statistical information about the electron. We can never calculate in advance what will be measured in a quantum system. We can only calculate the probability of obtaining a given measurement. Furthermore, Copenhagen tells us that this limit to what is predictable does not arise from the limitations of an imperfect quantum theory. It arises from limits of what is *knowable* by a perfect theory.

This idea was abhorrent to Schrödinger, de Broglie, and Einstein in particular, a source of smoldering dissatisfaction with the quantum theory. Copenhagen's assumed limit on what is knowable says physics is complete. Discovery is at an end and we cannot go beyond quantum mechanics in our understanding of matter. In practice, we can never, for example, predict when a radioactive nucleus will decay or what the individual energies of its daughter nuclei will be. Quantum theory is the end of physical law. Einstein ridiculed this notion as “God playing dice with the universe.” (Bohr is said to have replied to this statement, “Why should Einstein tell God what to do?”)

Dice are a good analogy here. When we throw two dice, we

don't know what the roll will be, but we know its probability. We know that after a large number of rolls, the total number of outcomes of each possible roll will be in fixed proportions. But of course Einstein was a good classical physicist in that he knew that the use of probability by the dice thrower is an expression of the *ignorance* of the dice thrower. If you knew exactly what forces the dice thrower's hand were to exert on each die, if you knew the initial positions and velocities of both dice, and if you knew distance to the table, then you could *predict* the outcome of the roll. This expectation dated from the time of Newton, when it seemed the motion of every particle in the universe could be predicted for eternity. The only limit to the precision of our knowledge about the future of any such particle would come from how well we knew its current state of motion. Physical law has always provided the mathematics to predict the future state of motion of any object provided only that its state of motion at any one instant be known. From such a snapshot in time, physical law lifts the veils of past and future.

The way physical law had operated for centuries inclined

many physicists to view the wave function as the imperfect tool of an imperfect theory. The knowability was a limit of the quantum theory. Einstein concluded that quantum mechanics was incomplete; a piece of the physics was still missing. But Bohr maintained that the uncertainty was fundamental, that there was nothing more to know and it would be forever impossible to predict the outcome of a quantum measurement.

Thus began one of the most profound scientific debates of all time, the debate between Bohr and Einstein over the interpretation of quantum mechanics and its completeness. Niels Bohr prevailed in that debate due to the brilliance of his arguments as well as his vociferous tenacity. It was a true clash of Titans because Einstein and Bohr were both founding fathers of the quantum theory, the world's two most revered physicists. Yet the final formulation of quantum mechanics, the theory that was verified in every experiment, still seemed incomplete to a community of physicists led by Einstein.

In the ensuing years, Einstein would raise various objections to quantum theory, usually concocted as “thought experiments.” Bohr, hearing that Einstein had exposed some inconsistency underlying quantum theory, would eagerly await each riddle. Working feverishly, he would show why Einstein's objections were ill-conceived or incorrect, if only viewed within the consistent framework of quantum theory. These debates also served to sharpen Bohr's conception of quantum theory. Bohr knew that if he could refute Einstein, the primacy of his conceptions would be established and humankind would be served by a consistent and coherent conception of reality. Bohr took it as his duty to carry the banner of the quantum theory and to argue it on its merits, without regard to sentimental ideas about an objective reality. Bohr would protect the new theory from the preconceived notions of a classical world. And he was successful.

Time and again Bohr would transmute Einstein's lead into quantum gold, strengthening the theory and its underpinnings, creating what was for him a masterpiece of logic and consistency. Bohr held no romantic notions about how nature should be. He was content to extrapolate about reality given only what was known or measurable. In this sense, he was much bolder than Einstein, willing to accept a physical reality at odds with both common sense and the trajectory of discovery previously established in physical law. Why assume the theory incomplete just because it is not in accordance with widely held notions of how nature *should* behave?

Einstein's most famous historical challenge to quantum mechanics was the EPR paradox, so-called for a paper authored by Einstein, Podolsky and Rosen. The crux of the EPR argument was that changes in the wave function can propagate faster than light. Based on the theory of relativity, it is accepted as axiomatic in physics that no signal can propagate faster than light speed. This notion is termed *causality,* that influences have causes. EPR described some elegant experiments for which quantum theory would predict instantaneous changes in the wave function, in violation of relativistic causality. EPR argued that *hidden variables* not taken into account in quantum theory must be present to rescue relativistic causality. These hidden variables would underly a more precise quantum theory. The present quantum theory was therefore incomplete since it did not account for these hidden variables.

But again, as he had done so many times before, Bohr

rescued the Copenhagen interpretation and established a consensus. He simply argued that the violation of relativity by the quantum theory had no **observable** consequences because the wave function was not **observable**. The quantum theory was complete. For example, we could not construct a communications system based on this breakdown of causality that would allow communications faster than the speed of light. There is no practical consequence of the non-causal behavior of the wave function.

For all the philosophical questions raised by the quantum theory about the objective reality and what is knowable, its mathematics paints an astonishingly successful picture of reality. For all the uncertainty about "interpretation", the quantitative predictions of the quantum theory are among the most precise in physical law. This quantitative success makes the quantum picture of reality hard to dismiss.

One great lesson, first realized by Heisenberg, is that material particles can travel from point A to point B without traversing the intervening distance. Bits of matter magically disappear and reappear at different locations. Also, bits of matter can travel multiple paths through space simultaneously. In a famous experiment where an electron is fired at a screen with two apertures, the data show the single electron apparently travels through *both* apertures.

Another great lesson is that what we know as matter, and the material world, is essentially empty space. The structure and hardness of matter owes itself to clouds of electron probability bound to an atomic nucleus. In fact, it is the wave nature of the electrons that allows matter as we know it to exist. The crack of a 90 mile per hour fastball when it strikes a swinging bat belies the fact that both ball and bat are fields of energy dancing in waves of probability on a sea of empty space.

Additional insight into the strange behavior of atomic processes is gained by considering an alternative mathematical paradigm to wave and matrix mechanics. The American physicist Richard Feynman was particularly gifted at coming up with diverse and creative approaches to understanding and describing physical law. His alternative picture of quantum mechanics is a real gem. Feynman was able to derive the

Schrödinger equation by assuming that a particle moving through space from point A to point B travels simultaneously over all possible paths through space *and* time. One of these virtual paths would be the shortest spatial distance between the two points, while another may involve travel backward in time or out to the edge of the universe before reaching point B. The probability waves of all possible paths combine together and interfere with each other such that the combination results in the path we may observe in an experiment.

Feynman's picture reinforces the message that the solidness of matter and its existence in space and time are illusions within a greater truth. The classical reality of certainty and causality rest on a quantum edifice. Below this edifice, they melt into a sea of quantum potential. Classical notions of the nature of existence do not survive in the quantum world. This quantum world is an intellectual abyss that humankind can never penetrate.

Some researchers did not give up searching for escape from the Copenhagen hegemony. One of these was David Bohm, who literally wrote the book on quantum theory. His text, *Quantum Theory* (1951), was an early classic. Before he weighed in on the Copenhagen interpretation of reality, he already made a famous discovery about the nature of quantum reality. Bohm was able to demonstrate the physical “reality” of the electromagnetic potential in the quantum theory.

The electromagnetic potential is a mathematical quantity from which the electric and magnetic fields can be derived. Knowing the potential, one can calculate the fields. Before Bohm's work it had been an article of faith in physics that the electromagnetic potentials were mere mathematical artifices with no connection to physical reality. It was assumed that only electric and magnetic fields could influence the motion of matter, but not their corresponding potentials. Bohm helped to show that unlike in classical electromagnetic theory, in quantum theory the electromagnetic potential is “real”. This means the mathematics of quantum theory describes instances in which the potential affects quantum systems, even when there is no effect from an electric or magnetic field. The electromagnetic potential, so long a mere mathematical artifice in the classical world, assumed its place in the quantum world among the "real" fields of the universe.

Originally from Wilkes-Barre, Pennsylvania, Bohm was an expatriate. A casualty of the red scare witch hunts of the early 1950's, he left the United States and ended up settling in Britain. As a young man he was influenced by Einstein, which led him to develop an alternative interpretation for quantum theory and the wave function.

In Bohm's picture the wave function is interpreted as a "real" physical field, a *quantum potential*, which affects the motion of material particles. Bohm considers the quantum potential similarly to the electromagnetic potential. They are both fields of force that ultimately affect the motion of particles. This view of a quantum potential is different than viewing the wave function as merely the reservoir of information *about* the particle. Treating the wave function as a field of force liberates the theory from the probability wave and the entire probabilistic interpretation of matter. God does not play dice in this interpretation of the wave function.

Bohm's theory hearkened back to the 1927 Solvay

Congress when de Broglie presented his pilot wave interpretation of the wave function. By 1928, de Broglie had acquiesced to Copenhagen, although he was destined to be born again after Bohm's 1952 paper[23]. In that paper, Bohm created a successful pilot wave interpretation for the quantum theory.

Einstein, de Broglie, and others could never reconcile themselves with the inescapable indeterminacy in physical law espoused under the Copenhagen interpretation. They did not believe in a limit to human knowledge. Bohm showed that there was no inherent indeterminacy accompanying the act of observation. The indeterminacy was merely a reflection of our *ability* to measure things. If our ability to measure things improved, human knowledge could expand into the regimes that Copenhagen said were impenetrable. It restored the promise of perfect knowledge of the future.

There is no indeterminacy associated with the collapse of the wave function in Bohm's theory. The equation for the wave function, still Schrödinger's equation, is assumed to be valid at all times, even when someone is **observing**. The act of human consciousness disappears from the mathematical formalism. **Observations** become observations again.

Bohm found a way, as Einstein had suggested, to describe the wave function in terms of hidden variables not present in the standard quantum theory. Any uncertainty about the outcome of any experiment would be just a natural consequence of how poorly we know the initial values of the extra variables. In this sense the Bohm theory is entirely classical. Deterministic equations hold for all systems at all times, as we are used to expecting from classical physics. There's no interpretation problem and consciousness does not affect matter. Nature obeys the same laws at all times independent of human observation.

Bohm didn't necessarily intend that his theory was *the* correct description of nature. He just wanted to show that there were alternative interpretations to Copenhagen. Bohm defended the principle of free and unfettered inquiry, believing that any overly restrictive interpretation would only serve to delay future discovery. For Bohm, calculation and prediction were mere engineering details. His real interest in physical law was in what it can tell humankind about the universe. Copenhagen set a limit on that knowledge that Bohm could not abide.

The pilot wave interpretation of the wave function, as a "real" physical field that can affect particle motion through an associated physical force, is quite interesting. In this picture, the wave function is some sort of ghostly influence in a super-dimensional space, an influence carrying the unrealized potential of all possibilities in space and time. This influence can reach through the dimensions into our "real" three dimensional world and influence material particles. It may yet be fair to call this influence, this field, this interpretation of the wave function, the pilot wave.

The competing interpretations of Copenhagen and Bohm have markedly different philosophical implications for the nature of reality. Copenhagen ascribes a causal, yet uncontrollable, influence of human consciousness on the motion of microscopic bodies. Bohm gives consciousness no special place in physical law, but posits the existence of a force field which pulls reality from a sea of possibility.

It is an amazing testament to the interpretative power of mathematical physical law that it could force upon its discoverers acceptance of a picture of the material reality completely at odds with anything the discoverers had ever known before. The pursuit of physical law has demanded acceptance of a reality which allows an electron to pass through two slits at once, allows the spontaneous creation of particles in empty space, allows a probability wave to travel faster than light, and allows a particle of matter to travel from point A to point B without traversing the intervening distance.

Perhaps the most revolutionary idea of quantum theory under the Copenhagen interpretation is the idea that there is no reality without an **observer**. Despite Bohr's victory in the interpretation battles of the quantum theory, the mathematics of the quantum theory is sullied by the need for the concept of **observation**. With Copenhagen, physical law has moved past the point of purely mathematical expression. Now the fields can change when a human makes an **observation**.

Whatever the truth or interpretation about mind and matter, the quantum theory has delivered an exuberantly magical picture of the material reality completely at odds with the expectations of common sense. If Neils Bohr is right, our quantitative mathematical understanding of the physical universe may be bound up with properties of human consciousness. The **observer** and the **observed** are parts of a single irreducible reality, just as Einstein discovered for space and time.

If David Bohm is right, then the pilot wave is an untapped reservoir of potential. Science and our understanding of physical law must progress to wield the pilot wave in the same way we now wield the electromagnetic field.

Does quantum theory reveal a link between mind and matter? Is the quantum theory the end of knowledge? Or is the quantum theory in the early stages of understanding the pilot wave? The quantum theory may approximate understanding of the pilot wave in the same way that Newton's law of gravity approximated the description of gravity before the discovery of general relativity.

Our search for physical law began as a quest for divine revelation in the natural world. The discoveries of physical law since its beginnings with Newton and Galileo have helped to push science away from any affinity with religion. But the culmination of physical law, the quantum theory, presents questions to us that may have only metaphysical answers. Perhaps it is time to reconcile mind and matter, science and spirit.

Spirit

The Age of Reason began with a new respect for the grandeur of truth. It was realized that beliefs about the universe can be verifiable, that faith is not the only servant of great truth. Human spiritual destiny springs from magnificent understanding of the physical universe. The price of this understanding is a brave recognition of the ultimate nature of truth:

> It is an ever-existing original, which every man can read. It cannot be forged; it cannot be counterfeited; it cannot be lost; it cannot be altered; it cannot be suppressed. It does not depend upon the will of man whether it shall be published or not; it publishes itself from one end of the earth to the other.[24]

There can be no human intermediary to truth. The proclamation of divine law is entrusted not to mortals but to the objective reality, the shared reality of direct experience. If the pursuit of mathematical physical law as the Word of the Creator is likened to a religion, then it is a rare religion in which the priesthood does not determine truth. Rather, truth is to be discovered, sought at the altar of repeatable experiment, kneeling to the objective reality.

The Creator could not rely on a man or a book to communicate a message of divine importance. What if the man is flawed? What if the book is lost? How will the people know the man is holy or that the book is true? We can let go faith in books and men because the Creator writes, godlike, across the canvas of the heavens. It is a message transcending eternity, wound into the very bodies of the creatures who dare to decipher it.

We may speak in English or Hebrew or Latin. Only the Creator writes π and G and c. Through mathematics we begin to understand the wonderful ways a Creator may find expression in the physical world of dust and bone, of force and field. These mathematical revelations are a gift of the spirit of reason.

The spirit of reason is fluid and flowering, growing and

changing. No generation is consigned to the dogma of their grandfathers. The understanding obtained by each generation is gifted to subsequent generations as provisional until the next great awakening, when the old truths emerge into a grand context.

The successive revelations of Force, Field, Spacetime, Evolution, and the Pilot Wave are *first principles* of physical law. They are first principles of our understanding of the physical world we inhabit, and all objective manifestations flow from them. Since spirit is linked to life, and life is linked to matter, the first principles of physical law must also be first principles of spiritual doctrine.

Force is the mathematical universe, an eternal design of divine expression, accessible to mortal Reason.

Field is the layered structure in the fabric of physical reality, overlapping oceans of force and energy which guide the motions and destinies of all things.

Spacetime is profound unification, the unification of space, time, and gravity, the unification of matter and energy.

Evolution is the expanding universe, the transformation of

matter since Creation. Among all the world's creation stories, the creation story of modern science is the most detailed, far-reaching, and imaginative. Staggering and awesome in its proportions, this creation story is evidenced by the cosmic background radiation and the recession of the distant galaxies.

Pilot Wave is the bizarre quantum reality that underlies the universe of human experience, a reality where matter is a dance of energy in empty space and where reality itself emerges from a sea of unrealized potential. The Pilot Wave is unique among the first principles. It hints at the end of physical law, the end of the growth of human understanding. It ties acts of human volition into the mathematics of physical law. But have we misinterpreted the meaning of the Pilot Wave? Do we really understand this matter field, this probability field?

The revolutions and revelations of Field, Spacetime, Evolution, and Pilot Wave all occurred within a span of 100 years. Now, the Copenhagen interpretation of the Pilot Wave is some 75 years old. We do not know whether the Pilot Wave is the end of physical law or the beginning of something wonderful, whether we are at the end of Newton's journey or pausing at the doorstep of a more profound understanding. Wherever mathematical physical law takes us, we are in dialog with our Creator, a dialog of profound spiritual implications.

Yet to speak of physical law in spiritual terms demands recognition that the human spirit yearns for so much more than a number. We feel questions and feelings deep within us that can never be expressed in mathematics. The quest to know and to understand arises from a deep emotional level. The drive to seek rational truth comes, ironically, from a level that transcends rationality.

When Amundsen or Magellan or Lewis and Clark set out on their voyages of discovery, they were driven by something deep within their humanity, something that transcended reason. Yet when they were on their voyages, they all navigated by the star of reason. They may have prayed for success, but they also took pains to plan and calculate for it. The miracles of their voyages were triumphs of reason over superstition. Great explorers of worlds seen and unseen approach divinity on a path through the objective reality.

Consider compassion, at the summit of every religion.

Compassion is ultimately objective, deriving in the uniquely human ability to project the subjective reality of another onto oneself. When the subjective realities of all creatures are assimilated into a single sustainable objective reality, it can mean peace for all.

Consider unity, the essence of spirituality. Unity is brotherhood among beings, acknowledgment of the single source of life. The mathematical revelation has been an unfolding story of unity, the divine quantification of oneness.

Consider humility, the source of tolerance and the effect of insight. Humility is to love all Creation as divine. Humility cannot abide the elevation of any part of Creation over another. The humility of Copernicus opened the door to the mathematical revelation. We could not have passed through that door believing literally in one chosen people among one chosen species on one chosen planet.

Copernican humility was at the heart of the Enlightenment and the Enlightenment was in the hearts of America's founding fathers. Washington, Jefferson, Adams, Hamilton, Madison, and Franklin all had something in common with their contemporary, Tom Paine: they were men of the Enlightenment. Like many people of learning during this time, their spiritual credo was *Deism.* A Deist recognizes no intervention by God in human affairs; superstition and ritual are replaced by reason.

Deism was the spiritual doctrine of the Enlightenment and of Tom Paine's *Age of Reason.* It was part of the suite of Enlightenment values from which The United States of America was born. The value of Christianity to the great experiment of American democracy was not in any literal supernatural truth, but in moral and cultural traditions which the founders thought held practical value for the organization and functioning of American society.

Even so, Deism is a recent and largely intellectual response to post-Enlightenment spiritual needs. There is no tradition, credo, or distinct path to spiritual growth espoused in Deistic terms. There is no Deist church. Rather, Deism is an umbrella term for an approach to spirituality which is self-defined, the ultimate conclusion of Luther's logic that no priesthood could intervene in one's relationship with God.

In cases like the evolution of life and the origin of the universe, the mathematical doctrine of physical law ultimately conflicted with the underlying European religious context in which physical law was developed. At the dawn of the 21st century, in the schools of the most advanced technological nation on earth, the objective truths of science continue to be challenged by religious authorities. The struggle to keep evolution from the minds of our children is a modern incarnation of the 500 year old struggle to keep the teachings of Copernicus from the minds of our ancestors. Religious fundamentalists today, as they did in the time of Galileo, fight to darken the light of scientific discovery where it conflicts with their ancient mythologies about the physical world. It is ironic that mathematical physical law, born in the cradle of Christian thought, should come into ultimate conflict with fundamentalists of that faith. Christianity was a chrysalis for the more profound spiritual understanding which must accompany the insights, the first principles, of mathematical physical law.

If physical law points to spiritual truth greater than the

Christian monotheism from which it was born, it also points us toward other ancient religious doctrines. There are many and varied religions in the world, reflecting the diverse histories and cultures of the peoples of earth. As an example of a religious doctrine in harmony with mathematical physical law, perhaps none is more striking than *Taoism*. The Taoists seem to have discovered the electromagnetic field thousands of years before Maxwell.

Taoism is an ancient tradition rooted equally in the spiritual and physical realms. The Enlightenment idea that spiritual doctrine must accord with the objective reality has been built into Taoism for 5000 years. Taoism places no spiritual importance on human personalities or dates or events. There is no guilt and punishment, no heaven and hell. Rather, there is only a single source of being: the Tao. The Tao is not a thing or a place or a person. It is neither good nor evil nor righteous. The Tao is simply *the Way*.

Where Western spiritual doctrines are relatively static, Taoism preaches unceasing change as the manifestation of the

Tao. The dance of creation itself is seen as timeless, but its face is ever changing. The Taoist is not offended to hear of probability waves or biological evolution or billion-year-old planets. It is all part of the Tao.

All things that rise from the Tao return to it: mountains, oceans, people, personalities. Nothing exists eternally separate from the Tao. All things are temporary manifestations of a timeless yet constantly changing interplay of *yin* and *yang*, the archetypal polar opposites epitomized by the Taoist symbol shown in the header. Each yin or yang manifestation of the Tao contains, at its strongest point, the seed of its opposite. A description of the Tao is like a description of electric forces as waves upon an electromagnetic sea, in flux and constantly changing.

The Taoists build their physical world from three elements. They say that human beings and human experience are only *vitality*, *energy*, and *spirit*. Vitality is the force of life. Energy is power and motion. Spirit is that which transcends the material world. The fiction of timeless matter, unmasked by the discoveries of physical law, is nowhere to be found in Taoism.

The elements of vitality, energy, and spirit are in constant flux, like the pilot wave or the electromagnetic field, like the interplay of yin and yang.[25]

The Western doctrine of mathematical physical law and the Taoist doctrine of vitality, energy, and spirit both find their expression and validation in the physical reality. They are not articles of faith. They are signposts to greater truth which are rooted in the experience of the individual. This is the essence of the spirit of reason: faith in the individual, faith in the objective reality.

Through this grounding in the objective reality of personal experience, Taoists discovered the electromagnetic reality underlying all human existence. Electrical processes provide the mechanism for action of mind and muscle. By the laws of electromagnetism, subtle energy flows accompany all electrical processes in the human body. The Taoists know the human bio-electric field as *chi,* a concept with counterparts in other Eastern traditions but which finds no analogy in Western spiritual traditions. This concept translates as *ki* in Japanese traditions and *prana* in Indian traditions. In these Eastern traditions, chi is understood as a manifestation of energy. It is the breath of life itself, an enormous reservoir of power accessible to adepts. The power of chi is the basis for ancient Chinese physical arts such as kung fu and tai chi, as well as for the healing arts of Chinese traditional medicine.

The objective reality of chi, and how it is linked to human spirituality, finds great example in the martial art of *aikido*. Developed in the early 20th century by Morihei Ueshiba in Japan, aikido literally means "way of ki harmony." Ueshiba described it as *the art of peace*.

Ueshiba was perhaps the world's greatest martial artist. He accomplished legendary feats even as an old man, pinning an opponent many times his size with a single finger or effortlessly avoiding any number of attackers. Aikido was an expression of his mastery of chi.

Ueshiba journeyed through many forms of martial art. He apprenticed to many masters and, in his early years, was something of a brigand and a mercenary. As his power and stature grew, his consciousness was transformed and he moved away from the negative aspects of the martial arts – hostility, violence, cruelty, and hate. He came to see that true *bushido*, the way of the warrior, is found in service of life. The ultimate warrior is a protector of life.[26]

Ueshiba discovered the techniques of aikido in the natural world – they were not invented. The techniques of aikido are expressions of love, love sufficient to protect a life under attack and sufficient to protect even the attacker. There are no blows taught in the pure forms of aikido. There are only techniques which mirror life and which protect life. Defense is not sought by wounding an adversary. Instead, the defender blends with the attack, takes control of the harmful energy unleashed by the attacker, and directs the energy toward an outlet that causes no harm to either defender or attacker. The confrontation ends with the attacker subdued and restrained, unharmed, by the defender. Ueshiba gave the world the ultimate martial art form, through which the awesome power of chi was directed in the service of love. Ueshiba's genius was to connect the physical reality of chi with the spiritual reality of love.

Taoism and mathematical physical law have some commonalities. Both are paths to higher truth rooted in the objective reality and in the experience of the individual. In both, the dance of form and energy is seen to be the temporal manifestation of an underlying unity, an underlying divinity. The prophets of Taoism and of mathematical physical law do not descend from a mountain with a message. Instead, they are people of genius who pull back a veil and expose an unseen mechanism, a hidden order. Their discoveries, their revelations, are shared equally among all people and need not be taken on faith – they are verifiable.

So it was with Newton, Maxwell, Einstein, Hubble, Heisenberg, Bohr, and many others. Their genius, their divinity, was not founded in supernatural circumstances but in eyes that see things others do not see, in minds that think what others have not thought. Like the spiritual epiphanies of reason, democracy, and tolerance, what such geniuses bring forth to humanity is an irreversible step higher, a step toward mortal comprehension of the divine truths which the Creator embedded into the physical universe for us to discover. Their discoveries are magnificent triumphs of heart and spirit.

The nature of the prophet has changed from that of a Moses

or a Mohammed to that of a Maxwell. No longer is an individual singled out by God to know truth, while vast multitudes are asked to accept truth secondhand and on faith. The modern prophet shows us truths expressed in the objective reality we all share.

So it was with the mathematical revelations that began with Newton. We had only to methodically and mathematically peel away the layers of the objective reality. Yet physical law took unexpected turns when the revelations of Force, Field, and Spacetime were subsumed by Bohr and the prophets of the Pilot Wave. Those quantum prophets were forced to develop an interpretation of objective reality when their discoveries of physical law outstripped intuitive human ability to comprehend the meaning of the mathematics.

With the quantum revelations of the early 20th century, our understanding of physical law and the nature of the universe changed dramatically. Newton, Maxwell, and Einstein all believed in a clockwork universe in which every bit of matter obeyed physical law – even if that law was as yet unknown to humankind. The equations of gravity, electricity, and magnetism apply to every bit of matter in the universe at all times. With a powerful enough computer, they thought, one could calculate the future. We now know that things are not so simple.

For one thing, many of the important equations of physical law cannot be solved exactly. Newton's laws applied to fluids, for example, contain a mathematical complexity that prohibits us from being able to predict the weather very far the future. There is a mathematical limit to what we can calculate or how far ahead we can predict the future.

More problematic, however, is the fundamental limit to human understanding that is built into Bohr's Copenhagen interpretation of the quantum theory. We can never predict, for example, when a particular atom of uranium will undergo radioactive decay; we can only calculate the relative fractions in a large population of decayed and undecayed atoms. There are things we can never know or calculate.

The equations of quantum physical law do not always hold for the uranium atoms or for anything else that can be measured. Specifically, the Schrödinger equation doesn't hold for an atom if a scientist should choose to try and measure something about that particular atom. Such a measurement collapses the wave function of the atom in an unpredictable way, in a way not described by the Schrödinger equation. Because of this element of choice on the part of the scientist, mind and matter are linked in the equations of the quantum theory in a way which did not occur with gravity, electricity, or magnetism.

To this day, physicists debate what this suspension of the Schrödinger equation during **observation** really means. We don't know if the apparent mind-matter connection is an artifact of our poor understanding of quantum phenomena, as Bohm suggested, or is a real effect of no practical importance, as argued under the Copenhagen interpretation. Recent experiments hint at a third interpretation: a real effect of potentially practical importance. It is clear that something has changed fundamentally in physical law and this change brings us to the doorstep of a mind-matter connection.

There is one well known mind-matter connection – the human brain. The material constitution of the brain is maintained by autonomous cellular processes. But major parts of the electric field of the human brain are controlled by the consciousness that resides within, by the *ghost in the machine*. Our memories, thoughts, and dreams produce a measurable electric signature. Indeed, the brain is a powerful electrical device which consumes up to a third of the body's energy.

During the course of a human life, the consciousness within evolves. At birth, human consciousness is protean and adaptive. Coordination of the physical body improves dramatically immediately after birth, with a corresponding change in the electrical patterns of the brain. It therefore seems natural that Taoisim holds evolution of consciousness to be the key to understanding our path of spiritual discovery.

Indeed, the revelations of mathematical physical law tell a story of universal evolution. Everything in the universe has been evolving since the beginning of time. Matter evolves. Planets evolve. Life evolves. The spiritual lesson of mathematical physical law, and of inclusive spiritual doctrines like Taoism, is that the spirit evolves too.

The physical universe evolved to become a platform for the

emergence and evolution of life. Life, in the form of human beings, supported the emergence and evolution of consciousness.

Matter forms a matrix for the evolution of consciousness. Once life is established, it organizes the matrix of its physical substrate to sustain itself. The actual atoms that constitute a human body change over time so that every several years or so the entire physical body is reconstituted. Yet something remains the same through these physical transformations. The living organism has an identity that transcends its physical makeup. The unity of purpose and form found in living beings leads us to expect that it is the way of nature for consciousness, once established, to sustain itself through changes in the underlying vehicle of life. Benjamin Franklin captured this expectation in his own articulate statement of Deist faith:

> When I observe that there is great frugality, as well as wisdom, in His works, since He has been evidently sparing both of labor and materials; for by the various wonderful inventions of propagation, He has provided for the continual peopling of the world with plants and animals, without being at the trouble of repeated creations; and by the natural reduction of compound substances to their original elements, capable of being employed in new compositions, He

> has prevented the necessity of creating new matter . . . When I see nothing annihilated, and not even a drop of water wasted, I cannot suspect the annihilation of souls, or believe, that He will suffer the daily waste of millions of minds ready made that now exist, and put Himself to the continual trouble of making new ones. Thus finding myself to exist in the world, I believe I shall, in some shape or other, always exist.[27]

In the threefold Taoist conception of human existence, comprising vitality, energy, and spirit, the energy flow of chi links the physical body to the spirit. Taoist spiritual growth begins with the mastery of chi and chi is in turn an element of the objective experience of the individual. This linkage between the objective reality of individual experience and spiritual enlightenment is absent in religions which do not demand a transformation of consciousness but which instead recognize mortal rite and ritual as a path to salvation.

We are fundamentally electromagnetic beings and we are continuously bathed in the electromagnetic fields of our environment, of other beings, of the earth, and of the sun. The physical manifestation of our consciousness is expressed through the electromagnetic field of the brain, which then drives electromagnetic responses in the motor functions of the body.

As consciousness emerges in each new human life, a new entity emerges in the electromagnetic field of the universe. The fruit of electromagnetic consciousness is born from the tree of human life. Taoism teaches that just as an apple, fully formed, may detach from the tree, so may consciousness evolve to exist independently of the human body. In the language of physical law, the Taoist doctrine of spiritual evolution implies that human consciousness can detach from the earthly vehicle of the human body and exist independently in the electromagnetic fields of the universe. It is a spiritual outlook in harmony with the first principles of physical law. The spiritual work of Taoism is to strengthen the energy body in service of spiritual development and transcendence of the physical body.

The teachings of Taoism are to make the adherent aware of the greater reality, to help navigate the journey of spiritual evolution. The Taoist trinity of vitality, energy, and spirit implicitly recognizes that life, the electromagnetic field, and spirit are aspects of the greater reality. Taoist teachings link the vitality of life and the energy of the electromagnetic field with the evolution of the human spirit.

Taoism is not a path; it is a way. It is a way in which our spiritual development weaves together threads grounded in the objective reality, in the physical universe.

Reason is a way, a way toward greater understanding and oneness with the universe. Through reason we bow to the material world and, in a stroke, we come to know it and gain power over it. The spiritual ascent of humanity began with faith, but it climbs through reason. Reason applied to politics is democracy. Applied to law, it is justice. Applied to understanding, it is science. The quantitative expression of reason is mathematics. All these gifts of reason are milestones on the road of human spiritual growth and it is through reason that we approach true divinity.

So when we speak of the Spirit of Reason, when we speak of the message of the Creator as inscribed in the physical world, we need not fear that this is an empty spirituality. The Spirit of Reason is as grand, as majestic, as sublime, as any spiritual tradition the earth has known. If we can let go as Copernicus let go and open the divine eye of reason, we will find the Creator living within us. All truths are to be found in the stars of the sky, the same sky we all share.

ACKNOWLEDGEMENTS

Thanks to Abraham Pais for his monumental scientific biographies of Bohr and Einstein. They provide priceless insight into the philosophical torment and rapture attending the development of 20th century mathematical physical law.

Edited by Dr. Neil Rand

Cover art created with the *GNU Image Manipulation Program v1.2*

Print layout created with *OpenOffice.org v1.1.0*

Printed in the USA by *Central Plains Book Mfg.*

Bibliography

Bohm, David. (1952) *A Suggested Interpretation in Terms of "Hidden Variables": Part I and Part II*. Physical Review, vol. 85, pp. 166-179 and pp. 180-193.

Cleary, Thomas, editor and translator, (1991) *Vitality, Energy, Spirit: A Taoist Sourcebook*. Boston: Shambhala.

Goldman, Martin. (1983) *The Demon in the Aether: The Story of James Clerk Maxwell*. Edinburgh: Paul Harris Publishing, in association with Adam Hilger Ltd.

Holms, John P., and Karin Baji, ed., (1999) *Bite-Size Ben Franklin,* New York: Saint Martin's Press.

Newton, Isaac. (1686) *Philosophiae Naturalis Principia Mathematica*. Translated by Andrew Motte, 1729, revised by Florian Cajori. Berkeley: University of California Press, 1947.

Paine, Thomas. (1794) *The Age of Reason*. Reprinted by Citadel Press: New York, 1988.

Pais, Abraham. (1991) *Niels Bohr's Times, in Physics, Philosophy, and Polity*. Oxford: Clarendon Press.

Pais, Abraham. (1982) *Subtle is the Lord... The Science and the Life of Albert Einstein*. Oxford and New York: Oxford University Press.

Stevens, John. (1987) *Abundant peace: the biography of Morihei Ueshiba, founder of Aikido*. Boston: Shambhala.

Wheeler, J.A., and W.H. Zurek, editors. (1983) *Quantum Theory and Measurement*. Princeton: Princeton University Press.

Notes

frontispiece quote: Paine, *Age of Reason*, p. 68, Defining the True Revelation.

1. Paine, *Age of Reason*, p. 69, Defining the True Revelation.

2. Ibid., p. 73, True Theology and That of Superstition.

3. Newton, *Principia Mathematica*, Mott/Cajori, p. xviii, Author's preface to the first edition.

4. Goldman, *Demon in the Aether*, p. 27

5. Ibid., p. 194

6. Ibid., p. 87

7. source unknown

8. Pais, *Subtle is the Lord*, p. 37-38

9. Ibid., p. 37

10. Ibid., p. 30

11. Ibid., p. 319

12. Pais, *Niels Bohr's Times*, (used with permission of the publisher) p. 384

13. Ibid., p. 299

14. Ibid., p. 253

15. Ibid., dedication page

16. Ibid., p. 296

17. Ibid., p. 308

18. Ibid., pp. 298-299

19. Ibid., p. 386

20. Ibid, p. 239

21. Ibid, p. 316

22. Ibid, p. 269

23. Bohm, *Physical Review* (1952)

24. Paine, *Age of Reason*, p. 69, Defining the True Revelation.

25. Cleary, *Vitality, Energy, Spirit,* p. 74, Sayings of Ancestor Lü

26. Stevens, *Abundant Peace,* for a history of Ueshiba and aikido

27. Holms and Baji, Bite-Size Ben Franklin, p. 18

INDEX

In the very beginnings of science, the parsons, who managed things then,

Being handy with hammer and chisel, made gods in likeness of men,

Till Commerce arose, and at length some men of exceptional power,

Supplanted both demons and gods by the atoms, which last to this hour . . .

– JCM

For information, lectures, education,
or to order another copy of

The Spirit of Reason

link to: **www.konfluence.org/press**

email: press@konfluence.org

mail:
Konfluence Press
P.O. Box 467
Manitou Springs, CO
80829

Konfluence Press
is a division of
Konfluence Research Institute